Through Gates of Fire

Also by Martin Bell

In Harm's Way
An Accidental MP

Through Gates of Fire

A JOURNEY INTO WORLD DISORDER

MARTIN BELL

Weidenfeld & Nicolson
LONDON

First published in Great Britain in 2003
by Weidenfeld & Nicolson

© 2003 Martin Bell

Third impression October 2003

A CIP catalogue record for this book
is available from the British Library.

ISBN 0 297 84748 1

Typeset by Selwood Systems, Midsomer Norton

Printed and bound in Great Britain by
Butler & Tanner Ltd, Frome and London

Weidenfeld & Nicolson

The Orion Publishing Group Ltd
Orion House
5 Upper Saint Martin's Lane
London, WC2H 9EA

To Major Richard Taylor and D Squadron,
The Household Cavalry Regiment

Contents

Introduction

This is a time for storm warnings if ever there was one. Some of those storms, of war and terrorism, are already breaking over us. We worry ourselves to bits about little and local issues – footpaths, flight paths, career paths and the like – as if the conditions of peace and freedom, on which our societies depend for their normal functioning, are natural entitlements, which can safely be taken for granted. This is the illusion that leads us to believe that we have no enemy at the gates and can safely ignore the world beyond our borders.

Don't count on it. We could be most dangerously mistaken. It is when war becomes a local issue that we really will have something to worry about. And it is worth remembering that in the end war always *is* a local issue, claiming individual lives in specific places. It is the trench or cellar or street or field where its victims, soldiers or civilians, breathe their last. It is the pilot who says, 'I didn't know who was there. I really didn't care. You fall totally into execute mode and kill the target.'[1] It is the rendezvous with death at some disputed barricade. When I see the dead and the way they are dressed – and you can spot the refugees by their layers of clothing – I want to know as a journalist how they died and who killed them and for what reason. I also wonder, in a there-but-for-the-grace-of-God sort of way as a co-inhabitant of the planet, *What were they thinking when they put those clothes on this morning?* Lieutenant Colonel Tim Collins, the controversial Commanding Officer of the 1st Royal Irish Regiment, expressed the same thought in his extraordinary, best-of-British speech to his troops on the eve of the war in Iraq in 2003: 'If there are casualties of war, then remember that when they woke up and got dressed that morning they did not intend to die this day. Allow them dignity in death. Bury them properly and mark their graves.' The Colonel added, 'It is a big step to take another human life. It is not to be done lightly. I know of men who have taken life needlessly in other conflicts. I can assure you that they live with the mark of Cain upon them.' The reality of warfare is that it is random and brutal. There is not a single damned redeeming thing about it.

It is only human to hanker for a golden age; but am I alone in noticing that golden ages are invariably assigned to times past, and that the people lucky enough to live in them are never aware of their contemporary good fortune? So it is with us. I am convinced that, if we don't blow ourselves into oblivion in the quest for regime change, or whatever other military adventures attract our leaders, and if we don't continue to go to war for its own sake, then future generations will look back on life in the Western democracies at the start of the twenty-first century, at least until 11 September 2001, as a sort of golden age, or fools' paradise – depending on the strength of the hostile forces ranged against us. From where I have been and what I have seen, my antennae tell me that the fools' paradise theory is very much nearer the mark. The Second Gulf War, an exercise of raw power that applied the values of the Wild West to the relations between states, has sharpened the edge of this argument.

There are things that happen and change your life through sheer force and impact. One of mine was being mortared in Sarajevo. But shocking experiences are not confined to war zones; another, as an MP, was being a witness of Parliament's failure to regulate itself – and not only as an observer but as an accomplice, as I shall confess. A third shock was being a witness to injustice in the International Criminal Tribunal at The Hague. Yet another was the Sally Clark case: Sally, a constituent, was a victim of the legal system and wrongly convicted for the murder of her infants. There were many other shocks, both at home and abroad. They included, more recently, a visit to the refrigerated warehouse in Tuzla where 4,500 victims of the Srebrenica massacre were stacked in body bags up to the ceiling awaiting identification and burial. Every one of those deaths was preventable. It was at that point that it occurred to me that, just as the United Nations has a Lessons Learned Department, so perhaps could journalists, politicians and just about everyone else, whether in or out of the public eye, have one. That's what this book is about. It is about thinking through what I have lived through – because if not, what's the point?

It is post-biography, if such a category exists, and derives from front-line experience of war and politics and news. We live in an age of overkill and times of the utmost peril – the most dangerous since 1945. We didn't need the Second Gulf War to tell us that, but it told us anyway, in unmistakable terms. According to the best estimate that we have, there are 693 million small arms in circulation. That works out at a hand-held killing machine for every ten people on earth. It is a planet we share with creatures who are in every respect less destructive than we are. With a few exceptions, the fiercest predator or most venomous reptile kills only one at a time, for food or in self-defence, and is benign in relation to man.

We kill our own more than any other species on earth, and we do it to the point of genocide. In the ratio of civilian to military casualties, the wars in the collapsed states of the late twentieth and early twenty-first centuries have mocked the Geneva Conventions and victimized the innocent to an unprecedented degree. In Croatia and Bosnia I have seen battles fought across the no-man's-land of cemeteries, tombs defaced and graves obliterated by cannon fire and tanks. This is a world in which it isn't even safe to be dead.

Weapons of mass destruction proliferate – and not only those in the hands of sovereign or rogue states. A passenger jet flown into a skyscraper is as much a weapon of mass destruction as a nuclear warhead. So is a sea mine rolled downhill into a village, or a 500 pound aircraft bomb bolted to a rocket and fired into a crowded city centre, or a mortar bomb aimed at a market place. These are not imagined examples. I have seen their effects at first hand. The Cold War was safer than this. Welcome to the pornography of war. The newsreader announces in hushed tones of awe: 'The B1 drops four 2,000 pound satellite-guided JDAM bunker-busting bombs.'[2] The makers of precision-guided bombs and missiles – which are actually not as precise as they are described to be in the manufacturer's catalogue – are replenishing their stocks in a seller's market. There is a shortage of Tomahawk cruise missiles. 'Now thrive the armourers ...'[3]

Our way of life is defended by new and ever more ingenious ways of death. The sole remaining superpower seeks out its enemies and blasts them with the firepower of its missiles, drones, long-range bombers and carrier-based aircraft. By answering terror with counter-terror, it bids for the status of the world's most hated nation. Too bad about the collateral damage and the needless taking of life. The higher the warplanes fly, the harder it is for their pilots to distinguish between a friend and a foe, an allied and an enemy reconnaissance vehicle (Iraq), a tank and a tractor (Kosovo), a terrorist cell and a wedding party (Afghanistan). The mark of Cain is upon *us*.

Language is another casualty. When we speak of degrading an enemy's assets, what we actually mean is killing people – the unarmed and the armed, the innocent and the guilty, blown to bits in the same high-explosive inferno. The same applies to 'blue on blue' or 'friendly fire' – the code for attacking our allies. Power and ignorance, like officers and maps, are a dangerous combination.

The United Nations, the last best hope of mankind, is a forlorn cave of winds on New York's First Avenue – invoked when it is convenient to do so and bypassed when it isn't. The most vital issues of war and peace are resolved in something

close to a state of anarchy. The rule of international law is
whatever the White House, with an obedient echo from
Downing Street, says that it is in the New American Century.
'If we need to act we will act,' said President Bush, 'and we
don't need the approval of the United Nations to do so.' The war
in Iraq, waged without a specific or sufficient United Nations
mandate, was the sort of imperial enterprise that, in the sweep
of history, belonged more to the nineteenth than the twenty-
first century. It was gunboat diplomacy, conducted not with
ships' cannons, but with all the weapons of mass destruction
that the science of the new millennium can procure.

None of the new world order comes cost-free. 'We have
entered the twenty-first century,' Kofi Annan reminded us,
'through gates of fire.' Across the world our citizens are now
the targets of reprisals by terrorists and mass murderers as never
before. Our governments provoke these assaults and act as
the suicide bombers' recruiting agency. They fail to meet their
obligations even as occupying powers.

Almost daily across four continents, the 'martyrdom missions'
multiply and claim more victims. A gaping hole in the New
York skyline reminds us of an implacable adversary hell-bent on
the destruction of our societies. Our 'ally' responds by chaining
suspects to trolleys and undermining the values it claims to
defend. Our media, which should be informing us, are instead
turning out the light and joining the stampede from reality in
the blind and mad pursuit of commercial advantage, of profit
without honour. The culture of celebrity, like an army of ants,
has colonized the news pages both tabloid and broadsheet. That
raises the question: when Armageddon threatens, isn't it time –
even past time – to work out what, in the sum of things, is the
relative news value of a weather person's love life or a footballer's grazed eyebrow? It's usually the same weather person.
And it's always the same footballer: he should have a newspaper
all of his own – the *Daily Beckham*. The England football
captain is rewarded for his ability to score improbable goals by

having more nonsense written about him than anyone else in the country.

Television is the god that failed. The US Army used to have an effective recruiting slogan: 'Be the best that you can be.' TV has not yet become the worst that it can be, but it is working hard on the project and is still on a downward trajectory. Just when you think it has hit the bottom, it finds new depths to plumb. The outcome is that it serves us less as a window on the world than as a barrier to it. Its screen is only a screen in the original sense – something that blocks our view of what lies on the other side of it. 'Oh my God!' we say to each other, and 'How terrible!' as the images of battle cascade into our living rooms from Iraq, or of atrocity from Mombasa or Bali or Casablanca . . . and then, because we find these things strangely unreal (and they have already been censored by the 'good taste brigade' of broadcasting to stop them upsetting us too much), we take refuge in 'reality TV' and the bromides of *Big Brother*. Our reach has exceeded our grasp. Something is seriously out of joint here. We are left with no heroes, but only celebrities. We need a survival strategy, but seem to lack enough of what it takes to put one together – understanding, courage, compassion, common sense, connectedness, care for each other, steadiness under fire and memory.

What follows is a journey through the new world disorder. Better fasten your seat belts. This could be a rough ride.

1

The Clash of Arms

Wars without Mercy

'Here's to genocide!' I murmured, raising a glass and lurking subversively in a corner of the balcony of the Imperial War Museum.

The museum, where wars are remembered without being glorified, is one of the world's best places to inspect the past and learn from it. Down below, as if on parade, stood the weapons of recent history, more resplendent in retirement than they ever were in use – tanks, rockets, artillery, aircraft and even a miniature submarine – the military artefacts that belonged to earlier, simpler and perhaps more innocent times. Alongside them was a tribute to the poets of the Great War, entitled 'Anthem for Doomed Youth' after Wilfred Owen's immortal elegy. Upstairs in the newest gallery, like the ghost in the attic, the museum was haunted by a brave attempt to show what happened next, after those wars ended. It was called 'Crimes Against Humanity' and was an exhibition without exhibits. It had to be. What was the point of filling a room with a selection of the bloodstains, clubs, axes, machetes and Kalashnikovs that have made our age the most murderous in human history? Instead the producers settled for a thirty-minute videotape on a loop, showing the killing fields of the twentieth century from Poland to Cambodia and Rwanda to Bosnia. The story told itself. It needed no fanfare to launch it – still less a drinks party.

The soundtrack accompanying the video included the comments of various witnesses to the crimes of our times – Michael

Ignatieff, Fergal Keane and myself, among others. It was Michael Ignatieff, who has studied these things with polymathic passion and commitment, who provided a chilling statistic: 'What is interesting about twentieth-century killing on the battlefield is that in the First World War 90 per cent of the casualties appear to have been soldiers. By the end of the century 90 per cent of the casualties were civilians.'

What an achievement that was! The century that gave us the jet engine and the spaceship, Picasso and penicillin, the cures to previously incurable diseases, great symphonies and poems and paintings, the end of empires and at least the idea of international justice, unimagined achievements in art and science – that same century, and some of those same scientific advances, equipped man for the first time in history to kill his own kind on an industrial scale. This he has been doing systematically ever since and regardless of the consequences, occasionally trying to outlaw some weapons, such as the anti-personnel mine, while developing others, such as the cluster bomb, which is an aerially dropped version of the same munitions and claims lives on a greater scale.

Both cluster bombs and depleted-uranium munitions were deployed by the British and Americans, supposedly in the cause of peace, in the Second Gulf War of 2003. Civilian casualties were inevitable, especially in built-up areas. We could hardly claim the moral high ground and at the same time drop cluster bombs around it.

An audit of the costs of war is illuminating, and daunting to those who believe in human progress. Compare two of history's prime examples of armed conflict on German soil. At the Battle of Blenheim in 1704, one of the bloodiest encounters of the eighteenth century, the total of British, French and Bavarian troops killed was less than half the number of Germans who died in the Allied fire-bombing of the city of Dresden in February 1945. Dresden was left with 42.8 cubic metres of rubble for every surviving inhabitant. Most of those victims were unarmed and defenceless; they were civilians and refugees, killed by the lethal combination of incendiary bombs and high winds. The same hellfire happened in Hamburg in July 1943. 'Behind collapsing façades the flames shot up as high as houses, rolled like a tidal wave through the streets at a speed of over 150 kilometres an hour, spun across open squares in strange rhythms like rolling cylinders of fire.'[1] Those were weapons of mass destruction in the early days. Their development has proceeded apace since then, and is still progressing, if progress is the right word for it.

One starlit night in the Iraqi desert in February 1991 I watched in awe as a barrage from the British Army's newly acquired multi-barrelled rocket launchers – a refinement of the old Soviet Stalin Organ – rained a high explosive inferno on the Iraqi-held ridgeline ahead of us. I was quaking that night because the ground under my boots was quaking. Brigadier Patrick Cordingley, commanding the British 7th Armoured Brigade, had called in a heavier concentration of firepower than had ever before been available to a British commander on a field of battle, even in the barrages and mineshafts of the First World War. He did it because he had no choice politically but to minimize the casualties on his own side, at whatever cost to the other. 'Poor bastards,' he said, 'I can't help feeling sorry for them.' The surviving Iraqis, deserted by their officers, surrendered the next morning. The Regimental Sergeant Major of the Queen's Royal Irish Hussars rounded them up like a sheepdog, single-handed in his antique Ferret armoured car.

At least the objectives of that campaign were military; but the clean war fought in a desert is a rarity. We in the Western democracies like to think of ourselves as fighting where we have to in a straightforward fashion, while those ranged against us, or not so advanced as we are, fight less honourably against us and against each other. We play within the rules and our enemies do not – as if war were a game of cricket in which we set the boundaries. We delude ourselves. The real distinction is between the types of conflict. Only two of them remain in the twenty-first century – the wars of collapsed states and the wars of international enforcement. If I were still a soldier, I would probably call them WCSs and WIEs – oh, how the military loves its TLAs, those three-letter acronyms! Sometimes one can mutate into the other, as when the Bosnian Muslims and Kosovo Albanians successfully provoked NATO, at different times, into attacking their enemies the Serbs on behalf of the international community. But the categories of warfare are distinct.

The wars of collapsed states, in which civil wars and wars of external aggression ferment in the same cauldron, are essentially about civilians and flags. Societies and governments disintegrate, civilians are not just caught in the crossfire, but targeted deliberately as a matter of policy. The idea of honour in armed conflict has vanished from the field like a ghost of the past. Today's wars are waged with the specific purpose of separating populations, driving one people from its homes in order to make a formerly shared territory safe for another people under a talismanic strip of coloured cloth. The most recent examples are Balkan and African, but there is a history of something like it in the Middle East. One of my defeats as a journalist, through censorship and denial of access (and a nervous concern for my accreditation), was that I failed to report the fate of a Biblical village wiped from the map of Palestine by the Israelis in 1968. Armed force can both make history and obliterate it. And reporters can lose their nerve.

The wars of international enforcement, by contrast, are attempts to impose peace and a new world order – with the suspicion of an economic dividend for the coalition waging them. They are American-led, with a degree of UN authorization which is either substantial (the First Gulf War in 1991) or gossamer thin (the Second Gulf War in 2003). Each form of warfare comes armed with its own euphemisms. *Theirs* is ethnic cleansing, *ours* is collateral damage; these do what euphemisms always do, which is blind the perpetrator to the reality of what he's doing – the reality to the victim is only too bloody obvious.

Each form of warfare has its own ways of applying deadly force: *they* commit atrocities, *we* conduct surgical strikes; *they* violate the Geneva Conventions, *we* respect them; *they* have warring factions, *we* have regiments; *they* kill their enemy, *we* degrade his assets; *they* fight dirty, *we* fight clean.

Oh, really? That would be news to the families of the Serbs killed in NATO's destruction of the Belgrade TV station in 1999. It was not a military target and could not have been bombed without substantial loss of civilian life. The rationale for attacking it was that it had been broadcasting lies; but the answer to lies, as I observed in the House of Commons at the time, is not bombs but truths. Where there are wars there will usually be war crimes; no, not so many on one side as on another – there is an issue here of proportionality – but war crimes nonetheless.

Ethnic cleansing is one of them, and if you have ever wondered where the term comes from, the answer is that you will find it in the manuals of the old Yugoslav Army. After an attacking force had driven back its enemy, its mission was to 'cleanse' – the word is *čišćenje* – the battlefield of pockets of resistance, unexploded ordnance and whatever else still made the ground unsafe. Only in the late twentieth century was the term applied to civilian populations. The bombing of a television station was something of a novelty too, and an explosive way of achieving the sort of media blackout that the military prefers so that it can go about its business in the darkness. The Arab broadcaster, al-Jazeera, has been an American target of opportunity from Kabul to Baghdad.

I am not arguing that there is a moral equivalence between different forms of warfare. Clearly there is not. What I am arguing is that we are all in this together; and campaigns of international enforcement, if conducted with genuine UN authority and within the accepted rules of armed conflict, can be used to prevent or limit the bloodshed in the wars of collapsed states. That is unlikely to happen, given the unprecedented dominance of the United States, unless the intervention is perceived to be in the national interest of the world's only remaining superpower. Recent history suggests that Pax Americana is more likely to prevail in countries with oilfields than in countries without them. That can be bad news for the countries without them, where the blood-letting continues – or the countries with them, where collateral damage continues to claim its victims.

Wars without Glory

It is an old soldiers' maxim that if you sit around waiting for bad things to happen, bad things will happen. Here is a real-world example – the fall of the Croatian town of Vukovar in 1991. It was a military campaign with a political and civilian objective. Like Dubrovnik, which was bombarded at the same time but not captured, Vukovar had survived the Second World War intact. It didn't survive the three-month siege by the Serbs, which so obliterated it that what had once been one of the glories of the Austro-Hungarian Empire looked, in the last assault, like Stalingrad by the Danube.

I dodged through the ruins with my friend and interpreter Vladimir Marjanovic, a sophisticated Serb who is a member of the Institute of Linguists and fluent in five languages (six, if you include Egyptian hieroglyphics). We had the written authority of the Yugoslav Army to report their victory; but it was a dangerous place in which to do the reporting. With cameraman Ian Pritchard, one of the BBC's quiet heroes, we sidestepped the bodies of the dead and the wild and drunken bands of roaming irregulars. Slivovic, the local plum brandy, was one of the fuels of the war machine. We looked around us to see if there was a single building left undamaged. There wasn't. A tree perhaps? Not that either. Not even a bush? No, not so much as a bush. A Serbian major estimated that in four months they had rained two million shells on the town, mostly mortars but heavy artillery too. They were making history by firing history – one of the shell cases dated from 1938. He was proud of that, although there seemed no point in saving a community by destroying it. The Americans had tried the same thing in Vietnam, to equally little effect. I observed in my last report from Vukovar: 'To the victor go the spoils – and the spoils are a heap of rubble.'

This is another novelty of our times. Wars over the centuries were partly, and sometimes principally, fought both for glory and for gain – for the loot and plunder that would gild the victory. Marlborough was richly rewarded for his triumphs, Wellington acquired an extra grand mansion and a triumphal arch that he hardly needed, and Nelson bickered endlessly over prize money. But that was before the development of weapons of mass destruction. It is a characteristic of the wars of collapsed states, that the havoc wrought in them is so total that *there are no prizes left worth fighting for.* This should be a deterrent to armed conflict, but seems to make no difference.

The Serbs in Vukovar invited us to the Croats' surrender in the outhouse of a vineyard. The delegate of the International Red Cross, Nicholas Borsinger, did his best to invoke the Geneva Conventions, and was later expelled for his pains. It was immediately apparent that his interpreter was not equal to the task, so I lent him the multilingual Vladimir. The Croats radioed Zagreb for permission to surrender. Zagreb didn't answer. They had no option but to surrender anyway. The Croatian commander had been ordered to fight to the last, and after his surrender the Zagreb government would not have him back. He spent the rest of the war in a Serbian jail. The scene that afternoon was a tragic microcosm of modern warfare. I hope that the video still exists. It should be required viewing for all political leaders who might wish to exploit the courage of their soldiers in uniform, or who see themselves as commanders-in-chief. In a grey November mist the thousands of survivors – those who could walk – shuffled past the ruins under armed guard. The men laid down their weapons in a pile at the feet of the conquering Serbs. They were broken-down old weapons, and come to that, they were broken-down old men. The sniper rifles had been buried; to have been seen carrying one of them would have meant certain death. It was a defining moment of the Balkan wars, but the straggling column of defeated people was an image so powerful that it reduced me to silence. I should have interviewed them but had nothing to ask them – not even the reporter's standby question-of-last-resort, 'How do you feel?', which, with a catch in my throat, I could not bring myself to utter. Even journalists sometimes try to hold on to shreds of self-respect. The outcome that night on the BBC was a mismatch between the most eloquent pictures and words that, if they hadn't lost the plot, were manifestly unequal to it.

There were other survivors, 250 men of military age, many of them civilians and medical staff, who sought refuge in Vukovar Hospital. Some were wounded; one was the Radio Vukovar reporter. They were all entitled to protection under the Geneva Conventions. Instead they were herded away by the Serbs out of sight of the cameras, executed in cold blood and buried in a mass grave at Ovcara on the outskirts of the town. It was one of the worst crimes of the Balkan wars. The truth about it was suspected immediately but not known in detail for years. Major Veselin Sljivancanin of the Yugoslav Army, a tall mustachioed and angry martinet, denied the Red Cross access to the hospital because, he said, some of the men sheltering there had shot his soldiers. He was later indicted by the Hague Tribunal, and went into hiding for as long as his luck held out. After twelve years, on 13 June 2003, he was arrested by the Serbian special police in Belgrade and handed over to the Hague Tribunal. The price on his head was $110 million in American aid.

Why does it matter now? It matters because war crimes matter, especially in a world where wars are more about civilians than about soldiers; and where in the long term the warlords themselves, hunted and hated, join the ranks of the victims of their crimes. Both sides made use of the images of the surrender –

the Serbs to celebrate their victory and the Croats to parade their defeat. Here is a truth of battle that isn't sufficiently noted, if it's noted at all. That is because, like many truths, it is unsettling and inconvenient. It is that, through the transforming power of public opinion and the televised images of violence, the winners lose and the losers win. That may seem paradoxical, but it is actually what happens. It did in the Tet offensive in Vietnam in 1968 and in the siege of Sarajevo in 1995. It did in the battering of Vukovar and Dubrovnik in 1991. The Croats, who had limited reserves of armour and artillery from a captured Yugoslav barracks, chose not to use either of them to break the siege of their beleaguered people. We found an artillery round marked 'Vukovar' six months later after a failed Croatian offensive in Herzegovina, but it was never used on the Danube. It suited the Croats to sacrifice their own and to play the card of victimhood. They understood the strength that lies in weakness. The political and military leaders in all these wars were as willing to inflict suffering on their own people as on their enemy. They would then display that suffering as evidence that they were the victims of aggression.

The card of victimhood worked. The Croats used the fate of Vukovar and Dubrovnik to argue for the recognition of their country by the European Council of Ministers at a crucial meeting in Brussels three weeks later. The Germans backed them. The British were reluctant, but were won round after having been offered a concession by the Germans, ten days earlier, on the opt-out clauses of the Maastricht Treaty. These clauses made it easier for John Major to sell the Treaty to his party in the House of Commons. It was also a shameful trade-off that ignited another war, as Lord Carrington, who was then the principal European mediator, had warned that it would. It left Bosnia next in line to be fought for by its three constituent peoples. The war cost 200,000 lives and made two million homeless. *Did we really abandon the Bosnians to their fate for the political expediency and convenience of the then ruling party at Westminster?* I believe that we did. I have looked for another explanation and cannot find one. Politics can be a dirty game, as I know, having seen it from the inside; but I had never imagined it could sink as low as that.

The Serbs plucked defeat from the jaws of victory. That had been their fate since the defining battle of Kosovo Field in 1389. Not all of them believed in the Vukovar enterprise anyway. I noted in my diary at the time, 'Some officers are much more peace-minded than the world gives them credit for, and deeply unhappy with the task entrusted to them.' By bombarding Dubrovnik and Vukovar they tarnished the reputation of a proud people. On the tenth anniversary of these events I addressed a conference of Croatian academics in Zagreb, and disappointed them by including the Serbs among the victims:

> There were no winners in this matter but only losers. In Vukovar the Croats lost a priceless part of their heritage which can never be retrieved. The Serbs inherited a ruin, which they annexed and occupied for a while and in due course handed back. They lost self-respect and gained nothing from it but grief. The best lesson to be drawn from it is a simple one, applying to all of us: lest we forget. The best homage we can pay to the past is to learn from it, and not to repeat its mistakes. The Germans have a phrase for it: *nie wieder* – never again.

Wars without Borders

Every armed conflict is unique to itself and fought in its own time and place – a more forward-looking term would be its own time and space, since the wars of the future will be conducted in what the military soothsayers describe as 'digitized battle-space'. I'll cross that bridge when I come to it; I prefer the known dangers of trenches and dugouts to the laser-guided perils of over-the-horizon hit squads. The point is that the one-off, stand-alone conflict, pitting one nation state's armed forces against another's, has become a thing of the past – except perhaps in the nightmare scenario of a nuclear war between India and Pakistan. The Falkland Islands War of 1982 was its last British example – as tragic but anachronistic as the football war between Honduras and El Salvador ten years earlier. (Salvadoran football supporters were set upon in Tegucigalpa, the Honduran capital, and the countries went to war.) The world is no safer since the wars of the nation-states ended; it is immeasurably more dangerous. War, like trade, is now globalized, with the same incalculable consequences. It feeds its own appetites. The United States, having defeated one enemy, seeks others within the time-frame of its electoral calendar. One of the features of an interconnected world is that its armed conflicts spill over into each other and its wars no longer have borders. In a single generation we have advanced from *jeux sans frontières* to *guerres sans frontières* – a global 'It's a Knockout'.

It was not in any war zone or trench line, but disembarking from a plane at Ottawa, which is just about the most peaceful city on earth, that I was struck with a Damascene force by some of the intersecting lessons of war – and by this overriding sense that *all conflicts are now international*. Lines on a map will not limit their reach or protect us from them.

The flags were straining in the slipstream of Arctic air that passes for springtime in Canada: they were flying at half-mast for four men of Princess Patricia's Canadian Light Infantry, killed two days earlier in Afghanistan, Canada's first war zone casualties since the Korean War. A distinguished figure in a less distinguished red windcheater (there was a lot of wind to cheat that day) parked his baggage trolley next to mine. He was General Jean de Chastelain, the senior soldier of their regiment, who for three years had supervised the faltering process of weapons decommissioning in Northern Ireland under the Good Friday Agreement. He was in Ottawa to attend the funerals, and I was there to give evidence in the trial of a Canadian citizen charged with kidnapping a Canadian officer in the course of the Bosnian war. The officer was also of the PCCLI – sometimes it seemed that the Canadian Army had only one deployable regiment. (Actually it had three, the others being the Royal Canadian Regiment and the Royal 22nd, the Quebecois 'Van Doos'.) The lessons were also in triplicate, extending to three countries, three continents and three conflicts.

The first lesson was from Afghanistan: *Smart weapons aren't as smart as they think they are*, by which I mean that if they hit the wrong target they will blow it to as many bits as if they hit the right one. Computerized warfare can be as dangerous to a friend as to an enemy. The four Canadian soldiers had died, half the world away from home, because the pilot of an American F16 mistook an allied night firing exercise near Kandahar for an al-Qaeda attack. 'I hope we did the right thing there,' he said, as he pulled away. In the same way, most of the British casualties in the Gulf War of 1991 were inflicted by 'friendly fire', including a clearly marked Warrior armoured vehicle of the Royal Regiment of Fusiliers destroyed by an American A10 tankbuster. It was the first war in history in which British soldiers had more to fear from their allies than from their adversaries. It was not the last, as the Royal Air Force and Household Cavalry Regiment learned to their cost in Iraq in 2003.

The second lesson was from Northern Ireland: *Things don't always go from bad to worse*. I have what the police call 'form' in Northern Ireland. I was in the first wave of metropolitan reporters to hit the Province in the late 60s and early 70s, witnessing pitched battles between the British Army and Loyalists on one side and Republicans on the other that seemed indistinguishable from outright war. If you survive firefights like those, you remember them, and the dates of some of them too – the Shankill on 11 October 1969 and Lenadoon Avenue on 9 July 1972. They were a crash course in what the Army calls FIBUA – fighting in a built-up area; and they were but a part of it. Over the years I was spat at, abused, physically set upon and threatened with being sent home in a box – by both sides, which was a sort of badge of neutrality if not a consolation. And it was in Belfast that I first acquired my taste for the company of warlords. Andy Tyrie and Billy MacCarroll of the Ulster Defence Association, where are you now in these quieter, gentler times? That they *are* quieter and gentler is, I hope, hardly deniable. Of course there are walkouts, political tantrums, suspensions of the Assembly and setbacks to the peace process; but there *is* a peace process, partly brought about by international pressure, but principally by the wish of the people to live at peace with each other. Men once dedicated to armed struggle reaffirm their commitment to the alternative. General de Chastelain has been an important and patient figure in it, for which I thanked him. The situation is light years better than it was a generation ago. It reminds us of conflicts which, if they cannot be resolved, can at least be managed until a resolution presents itself. Think of the Lebanon, El Salvador, Namibia, all of which are now at peace after having been locked in apparently endless strife. When the war in Lebanon was over, Muslims and Christians embraced each other across the no-man's-land that had divided them. After thirty years even Cyprus craves a settlement. Peace can be globalized as well as war.

The third lesson was from Bosnia: *Actions have consequences.* Especially today in an interconnected world, a world without borders, even local and limited actions can have the most catastrophic outcomes. The defendant in the Ottawa Superior Court, under a statute never previously invoked, was Nicholas Nikola Ribic of Edmonton. He was a Canadian of Serbian origin accused of having kidnapped a Canadian UN officer, Captain Patrick Rechner, in May 1995. It had been a critical phase of the war, in which for the first time the Serbs were losing ground to Muslims and Croats. NATO aircraft had bombed an arms depot in response to flagrant ceasefire violations by the Bosnian Serbs. Their television service had shown Captain Rechner handcuffed to the depot's lightning conductor. Two other unarmed UN observers, a Czech and a Russian, had been used as human shields in the same way. Three hundred and fifty UN soldiers had been held hostage across Serbian territory to deter further air strikes. My role at the Ribic trial was a minor one: to authenticate a TV report on the incident that was introduced as evidence. It included an intercepted radio message from the Serbs to General Rupert Smith in the UN Sarajevo Command: 'Three UN soldiers are now in the site of the warehouse. Any more bombing, they will be the first to go. Understand?' The speaker identified himself as a Bosnian Serb Army soldier. He didn't sound like one.

No lives had been lost. The UN hostages had eventually been released unharmed. Ribic had not in any case been a ringleader but a low-level functionary, known locally as 'the lumberjack'. His lawyers could argue that their client had acted in good faith and in the interests of peace, since his alleged action – even if it were admitted – had helped to prevent further bombings. The kidnappings, however, had had the most terrible and far-reaching consequences. There was no way that Ribic could have foreseen this, but they had led directly in a straight line of march to the Srebrenica massacre eighteen days later. Again, it was the international dimension of the problem, and the nationalities of the peacekeepers, that made all the difference.

The chain of events included a secret meeting on 4 June 1995 between General Bernard Janvier, the UN commander in Zagreb, and General Ratko Mladic, commander of the Bosnian Serb Army. A hundred and eleven of the hostages were released three days later, twenty-eight on 13 June and the remainder on 18 June following further meetings between the UN and the Serbs. Although they had obtained no formal agreement, the Serbs had believed that they had a firm understanding that, in exchange for the hostages' release, there would be no more bombing of their territory. 'We got a commitment of no more air strikes,' said their vice president Nikola Koljevic, 'no more hostile acts against the Serbs.'[2] The United Nations had returned to conventional peacekeeping, and the Serbs to unfinished business.

The unfinished business was in Srebrenica, the enclave established as one of six safe areas by a Security Council resolution two years earlier. The Bosnian government forces there were partially disarmed, and Muslims streamed into it from outlying settlements in the belief that UNPROFOR – it was called the UN Protection Force, wasn't it? – would protect them. But it didn't. The Serbs, emboldened by their hostage-taking, moved against it in the second week of July 1995. NATO air strikes were called off on five occasions, and the demoralized Dutch peacekeepers offered no resistance. The women, children and old men were taken out to Tuzla. The men of military age were either shot trying to escape across the front line – although a few got through – or executed in cold blood on playing fields and farms in the days that followed. More than 7,500 were killed. It was the worst war crime in Europe since the Second World War. The Serbs denied it even when it was proven. The response of General Mladic, who was not as hard to find as NATO supposed, was to stonewall: 'We don't talk about Srebrenica.' Their vice president, Nikola Koljevic, shot himself.

The *Wall Street Journal* reporter David Rohde, who wrote the definitive account of it, accused the United Nations of more than just standing aside when it could have resisted. Without the United Nations' presence the massacre would not have happened at all, or certainly not as it did happen: 'There is no need for thousands of skeletons to be strewn across eastern Bosnia. There is no need for thousands of Muslim children to be raised on stories of their fathers, grandfathers, uncles and brothers slaughtered by the Serbs. The fall of Srebrenica could have been prevented.'[3]

The British officer Major Milos Stankovic, who had been inside the UN chain of command, reached a harsher conclusion: 'Sure, the Serbs were the trigger-pullers at Srebrenica, but the international community loaded their magazines for them.'⁴

The blame lay not so much with the troops – although the Dutch must take a share of it – as with the governments. The British, French and Dutch, who were the main players in the UN force at the time, were unwilling to risk the lives of their own soldiers to save the lives of thousands of Bosnian Muslim civilians. They rated them on sliding scales of value. This was the mind-set of a post-heroic age that supported bombing from 15,000 feet, in Kosovo, Afghanistan, Iraq and elsewhere, to minimize *our* casualties at whatever cost to *theirs*. It was the mind-set that refused to deploy the armoured brigade in Rwanda, requested by the United Nations, that could have prevented genocide and saved half a million lives. It was the mind-set of ministers who declared in the House of Commons: 'Our overriding priority is the safety of British troops.' If that were so, the troops should have been kept out of harm's way on Salisbury Plain preparing for a war they would never have to fight since to do so would have compromised their precious safety. This attitude was not only craven and cowardly – it was contemptuous of the armed forces themselves. When they sign on to serve, and their officers accept the Queen's commission, they do not undertake to do so only in safe places; and if that were the deal on offer, they wouldn't take it.

Wars without End

Almost without exception the Western democracies are guided and governed in a war-torn world by a generation of leaders who have never heard a shot fired in anger. That is not to disparage them. It is an effect of the superpower condominium that maintained a global if not regional peace from 1945 to 1990. Our political leaders never knew the ardours of military service and their American counterparts, with honourable exceptions such as Senators Kerry and McCain, generally evaded it. The most aggressive are the so-called chicken-hawks –

old men advocating the sort of risks and sacrifices from which, as young men, they walked away. One result of this deficit of experience is an enthusiasm for military enterprises followed by a reluctance, when the chips are down and the costs are clear, to go through with them. Panic sets in: *Casualties ... No one ever told us about casualties ... I'm a politician, get me out of here.* This is sometimes known as 'crossing the Mogadishu line' – a reference to the American debacle in Somalia in 1993. On one occasion a senior British officer was shown the yellow card – nearly relieved of his command – for suggesting to a group of defence correspondents that if there was a war there would be casualties, and the British people should know that.

The issue is body bags, and the extreme aversion to casualties – our own casualties, not anyone else's – that prevails in the Western democracies. It is a relatively new phenomenon – as indeed are body bags themselves, which in earlier times weren't used at all, or were improvised from mattress covers. A concern about body bags never seems to have troubled the warrior Prime Minister Winston Churchill, an incorrigible embarker on costly expeditions, who ordered garrisons to fight to the last man and feared after the fall of Singapore that 'our soldiers are not as good fighters as their fathers were';[5] but it does trouble his successors, and it should. No man, not even a politician, should lightly send another into the line of fire.

Frederick the Great wrote to Voltaire in 1742, 'It is the fashion these days to make war, and presumably it will last a while yet.' The fashion hasn't changed, and it is safe to predict that it will last for a while longer. Man is an aggressive animal who, unless constrained, will seek to settle his differences through the barrel of a gun. It is past time therefore – isn't it? – to raise our eyes from the ground around our feet, to assess and confront the hostile forces ranged out there, to pre-empt armed conflict where possible and join with others in suppressing it where necessary. Either that, or we are doomed to a future bloodier than the past – and wasn't the past, in all conscience, bloody enough?

What mega-tonnage of a wake-up call do we need? Napoleon III is reputed to have said, 'The history of artillery is the history of progress in the sciences, and is therefore the history of civilization.' What would he have made of the chemical warhead, a most progressive form of artillery in the scientific sense? Progress in the sciences has got out of hand. Relative to where we stand now, Napoleon III lived and ruled and lost his battles in an age of primitive warfare. (It is an irony of history that his son, the Prince Imperial, was killed in fighting for the British against the Zulus.) Our weapons systems have increased our killing power exponentially, while human nature stays obstinately the same.

A few of the war-zone basics may come in handy. First, since the beginning of wisdom is to know how much we don't know, it is worth reflecting that we may be even deeper in the mire than we think we are. Second, we share the planet with people who are, in the matter of their humanity, indistinguishable from ourselves: human life is as precious in Bujumbura as in Basingstoke. Third, although with limited capabilities we cannot help everyone everywhere, it does not follow that we cannot help anyone anywhere. Fourth, we are not dealing with abstractions here, but with the actions of individuals for better or worse: *Good things happen because people make them happen and bad things happen because people let them happen.* Fifth, the United Nations is not there to be used when it suits us and bypassed when it doesn't: it is the shining city on the hill and the last, best hope that we have. Sixth, the 'mission creep' so remarked on by its critics is a fact of life in peacekeeping; a force will be sent to achieve an objective, and will find when it gets there that the situation has changed and the risks have increased. That is not of itself a reason to sacrifice the defenceless and creep away from the mission; there can, or should, be such a thing as honour in peacekeeping. Seventh, we do not have the option of turning our back on the world and hoping that if we leave it alone it will leave us alone. It will do nothing of the kind. It is an increasingly dangerous place. Whether we like it or not we shall have to bear the rising costs of living in it. Like soldiers stranded in no-man's-land, we have no other hole to go to.

2

The War of Words

Hits and Myths

For all that it deals with events and realities, television news has a prodigious capacity for myth-making. Like a huckster on the high street it hawks its wares regardless of their quality. Its multiplying channels compete for audiences and advertisers by promoting themselves as the hottest property in the global market place: 'Give us twenty-two minutes,' they boast, 'and we'll give you the world.' Actually it used to be closer to thirty minutes, but station breaks and self-promotions cut into more and more of the news time – not that it mattered to the media corporations, for which news is no more than product. The hype was there for a reason: it is a general rule of thumb that the orchestras of least distinction are those with the loudest trumpet sections.

One of the myths of the television industry is that it watches the world with an unblinking eye. CNN, which had the advantage of being the original rolling news service, believed its own propaganda about being first and fastest with the news. It encouraged the fiction to take hold that the Gulf War of 1991 was broadcast live as it happened. This was just not true. Apart from a short period in Baghdad under bombardment, nothing was shown live on any channel except correspondents addressing cameras at a safe distance from the front line. I know that, because I was actually on the front line, but able to broadcast only after a time delay for reasons of operational security. Those who knew didn't tell and those who told didn't know – as much in war reporting as in politics. The military guarded the barriers and controlled the battlefield. Within it we had no more freedom of movement than our colleagues in Iraq, although our reports were not introduced from London with the same health warnings of censorship as theirs; and such action reports as we filed, when a coalition of overwhelming force swept past the rout of a defeated army, were censored and satellited out of the desert between one and four days late.

That was the sort of time lapse we had taken for granted a generation earlier, but was supposed to have been made redundant by the new technology. Now it turned out that the new technology was no more immediate than the old – except for an element of cosmetic enhancement that owed more to graphics than to facts. The medium, having passed its first youth, had become – to put it bluntly – a bit of a tart.

If a network announced that it was cutting to a live report from the front, that usually meant the front of the International Airport Hotel in Dhahran – or more accurately the back of the hotel, the news being delivered by a crisply dressed person on a platform between the hospitality tent and the swimming pool. I knew a man who became famous for this. He was a young and good-looking Canadian who apparently had a following among the ladies. He reported for the American network NBC on some explosive development in the war during the half-time break in the Superbowl. The development was not shown, of course, but he was, and he made the most of it in all his safari-suited glory. The networks refer to such people – without irony, because Americans don't do irony – as 'the talent'. As the fan mail poured in from Iowa and Illinois, the talent of Dhahran became known for a few weeks as 'the Scud stud' – a title bestowed many years later on the BBC's Rageh Omaar.

This sort of stuff is palm-tree television and a mainstay of rolling news. It hijacks a patch of desert for use as a studio, and is easy enough to spot. If you see someone broadcasting with not a hair out of place, in a freshly pressed tropical outfit and against the backdrop of a palm tree, you can take it as a sure sign that the events being reported are over the horizon, the footage is acquired from an army or news agency, and the information is coming to you at second or third hand. Because of the dynamics of live television, some of it will be faxed or e-mailed from New York or London to the feed point. The rest will be spoken into the performer's earpiece right up to the time of transmission, or even during it. That is not journalism but puppetry. The network is a party to this deception, since it claims to be where the action is, and boasts – does it not? – of being the world's news leader. What it is not going to say is: 'Sorry, but we've failed to make it to the front line today; the news is coming to you from far behind the battlefield and we're not even runners-up.' The same applies to reporters on hotel rooftops. First-hand journalism is expensive, time-consuming and increasingly obstructed by censorship and denial of access. Different armies will give different reasons for putting up the shutters, from 'We can't guarantee your safety,' to 'Your accreditation is not in order,' 'The general is too busy to see you,' 'Sorry to disappoint you, but it's Ramadan,' and my all-time favourite, 'All journalists are spies.' (I like it so much because a few of them actually are.) The outcome is the same. The most effective form of censorship is the roadblock, now more than ever: all that it takes to block the news is a pole across the road.

Within the myth of the networks' all-seeing eye there lies a kernel of truth. Television is the most consequential medium ever to communicate events to people. It does more than hold a mirror up to nature. For all that its snapshots are fragmentary and sometimes misleading, generals plan and conduct their operations as if the ghost of the camera is hovering over their shoulders, especially in their degree of willingness to take and inflict casualties. The public-relations nightmare is not blood on the field but blood on the screen. One myth thus begets another: the myth of the casualty-free conflict. TV's focus on the human costs of war puts a premium on short, high-tech stand-off campaigns, using remote weapons like the daisy-cutter bomb and the Tomahawk cruise missile, with the involvement of ground troops kept to a minimum late in the campaign, like the US cavalry charging to the rescue in the last reel of an old movie. The victorious troops then disappear up the aircraft steps (there have been few troopships since the Falklands), leaving the politicians to reap the rewards and the locals to clear up the mess. This at least was the model until the Second Gulf War, which was also designed as a short campaign to end with a quick victory.

Wars and War Games

In the early 1990s the British Army became so concerned about this third force on the battlefield that they factored it into their war games. Although as an infantryman I never rose to a higher substantive rank than corporal – and history records that we ex-corporals are a dangerous lot – I was invited to the Staff College at Camberley to play the part of media intruder in the warfare of the late twentieth century. Since a war game at the command level is like an exercise without soldiers, I was the only other rank on the field of battle. It was conducted by colonels and brigadiers playing the commanders of Red and Blue forces (the Cold War models had not yet been discarded), with the aid of computer projections, sand-tables, maps – and, for the first time, television. The Blue side was a coalition of the willing, based on NATO, and the Red side was a rogue state with some kind of a composite African name, like Mozambia (the colonial model was also slow to expire). In one of the scenarios the Blue air force, aiming at a Red arms dump, destroyed an orphanage instead. My role was to subject the commanders to a heavy-duty grilling in a TV interview, accusing them of incompetence and a breach of the Geneva Conventions, and showing how it would look on the evening news. For added impact, we included file footage of smoking ruins, of which I happened to have a plentiful supply, as if from the scene of the attack. It didn't look good – not good at all. In fact it looked bloody dreadful. As we war-gamed the consequences, the coalition cracked under the strain and one of its partners defected.

The Army's concerns were prescient and not far ahead of their time. In the bombing of Kosovo and Serbia in the spring of 1999, NATO came close to losing the war of words with the Milosevic regime, and with it the whole campaign. This was the result of a series of targeting errors, usually on a Friday, including the destruction of the Chinese Embassy in Belgrade. In the House of Commons, I won no friends on the Labour benches by describing NATO as the gang that couldn't shoot straight, and suggesting a bombing pause on Fridays until whatever the problem was could be sorted out; but the parliamentary awkward squad, to which I belonged at the time, caused Downing Street less anxiety than the British press corps in Belgrade, including John Simpson and Jacky Rowland of the BBC, Julian Mannion of ITN and Robert Fisk of the *Independent*. They were reporting the effects of the bombing under the difficulties of danger, censorship and the anger of Serbs who saw all Western journalists as NATO's surrogates. Being caught in the crossfire between Alastair Campbell and Slobodan Milosevic in the no-man's-land of the media war was not an enviable predicament.

John Simpson bore the brunt of it because of his prominence; and at the same time, since it never rains but it pours, he had the painful experience of becoming the BBC's only casualty of the war by breaking his foot in the jacuzzi of the Grand Hyatt Hotel. I rallied to his cause as I usually do when he is in trouble, urging the government to understand that it was engaged not in a propaganda war but in the defence of certain values, including a free press and the right to be told uncomfortable truths. John is an odd bloke in many ways, charming yet remote. The longer you know him, the less you know him; but he is a straightforward old-fashioned reporter, and as far from being a natural subversive as anyone on the BBC's payroll. He doesn't even begin to qualify for membership of the awkward squad. He looks like an ambassador, and I suspect him of harbouring a sneaking ambition to become one. When we once shared a platform at a literary festival, he described himself – only half-jokingly, I think – as 'an establishment creep'. High-profile TV journalists have a tendency to put themselves down because they know very well that, if they don't, someone else will.

John's reporting touched a nerve in Downing Street, which dispatched its elite special forces in the form of Alastair Campbell, the Prime Minister's spokesman, to turn the tide of the media battle and sort out the NATO press office in Brussels. Mr Campbell said later, 'In the face of the aggressive media, you sometimes need aggression in return.' He complained of media bias against the alliance: 'What we were saying was liable to be attacked as "NATO propaganda", whereas the Serb day trips to the scene of the NATO crime were treated as the truthful exposé of a flawed air campaign ... After Iraq and Kosovo, the media needs to reflect whether it has not provided a kind of template to dictatorial regimes in how to use the Western media to their own advantage.' He attacked what he called 'the sneer squad' and replied in kind: 'The day of the dare-devil reporter who refuses to see the obstacles to getting the truth, and seeing it with his or her own eyes, seems to have died.'[1]

That was a bit rich, I thought, coming from a Whitehall warrior who would face no greater hazard in his daily routine than being hit by a number 48 bus while training in Hampstead for the London marathon, and who had never in his life set foot in a war zone, except once in Kosovo when the war was safely over. How many of his colleagues had Mr Campbell lost on front lines? How many of his friends had been blown away on a mountain road by an anti-tank round? How many of their funerals had he attended? How many of their relatives had he comforted in darkened rooms? What could he know of the sort of courage it would take to walk into Kosovo from Albania through unmarked minefields on the border and the prospect of ambushes beyond it? But his remarks were a sign that the government was rattled. Its concern seemed to be not so much humanitarian – that bombs were going astray and killing the innocent – as presentational – that they were *seen* to be going astray and killing the innocent on the evening news, with collateral damage to the alliance and its reputation. This is how war is waged in the satellite age. Television is not inert but active, a catalyst and dynamic agent of change. Perceptions shape realities as much as realities shape perceptions. An important element of modern warfare is the management of perceptions.

Jamie Shea, the NATO spokesman, observed somewhat ruefully that media campaigns don't win wars but they can certainly lose them: 'Modern warfare is characterized by the extreme inequalities of military technologies and the extreme equality of the public debate.'[2]

So it was that even the Alastair Campbell spin machine, serving the most persuasive prime minister of modern times – and the most Gladstonian since Gladstone – had the utmost difficulty making the case for war with Iraq in 2003, not only because of the lack of hard evidence of the weapons of mass destruction, but also because of the lack of compelling television pictures of human distress of the sort that enlisted support for the invasion of Kosovo in 1999. The British people saw what was on offer: a few images of empty warheads and a doctored dossier that copied the spelling mistakes in a thesis by a Californian academic – and refused to be persuaded. Before the war was launched, the proportion of its unconditional supporters in Britain fell for a while to a meagre 9 per cent. The Prime Minister's if-only-you-knew-what-I-know argument was never supported by hard information. Even US Secretary of State Colin Powell's presentation to the Security Council lacked the 'Adlai Stevenson moment' of the Cuban missile crisis, the decisive photograph that would make the case for armed force. So it was that a quarter of the British Army and a third of the Royal Air Force went to war without strong public support – and nothing like that had happened since the Suez debacle in 1956. The precedent was hardly encouraging, although the impact of television was not, in those days, one of the moving parts of democratic decision-making. It is now.

In March 2003, as six American carrier groups assembled in the Gulf and 200,000 American troops in Kuwait, the powerful images of the superpower's war machine, beamed around the world, actually made it harder to persuade the Security Council to authorize the use of force against Iraq. The rest of the world looked war in the eye, and flinched. I shall return to this phenomenon – a novel variant of the CNN effect – in my account of the war in Iraq (chapter 12). Suffice it to say, for the moment, that the BBC's correspondents in Baghdad were excoriated by the government spin machine for operating 'behind enemy lines'. One of them was even compared to Lord Haw-Haw, the Nazis' traitor of the airwaves. When those who govern us disagree with the message, they would still like to shoot – or preferably suffocate – the messenger.

If not always a force for peace, television is capable of making things a little less worse than they would have been without it. An example of this was Balkan prisoner exchanges. There was no more fallible transaction between the peoples and armies of Bosnia, and nothing that so brought out their distrust of each other, as the handing over of bodies, dead or alive. At an early point in the war the negotiators for both sides routinely came to ask for the presence of a foreign TV crew on the front line at the point of exchange, as a means for each to hold the other to the agreement they had reached. It didn't always work, but it did make failure less frequent and inevitable.

TV also acquired an original role as a substitute for armed conflict. There was a period after the Gulf War of 1991 when, as the cooler weather returned in October, the Americans and

Iraqis would regularly conduct a virtual war on either side of the border with Kuwait. The Iraqis would rattle the sabre of a division of their Republican Guard, the Americans would reinforce the Kuwaitis and mobilize their pre-positioned armour. Even the Royal Marines would show up, without armour or transport of their own, as a token of British resolve. The result was the theatre of war at its most benign. Television showed the tanks of both sides throwing up spectacular clouds of dust, and provided a backdrop for tough-talking commanders, celebrities in uniform for at least a couple of weeks. Saddam Hussein returned to his favourite showcase on the front page of *Newsweek*. The TV networks, which like nothing so much as a good, safe, time-limited crisis, cooperated. They not only reported it but validated it: if they fielded their star reporters on the Basra road, it *had* to be serious. Christiane Amanpour's presence clinched the argument. Both the Iraqis and the alliance talked a terrific war, using CNN and the BBC to blast their sound bites back and forth into each other's territory, to detonate harmlessly on TV screens in hotels and government offices. No damage was done, not a drop of blood was spilled and honour was duly satisfied. In the light of what happened twelve years later it was a strangely unreal encounter: what we could do with is more virtual war and less of the real thing.

After a few of these episodes, I knew the routine by heart and could sleepwalk my way through it: tumble off the plane and into the press centre in Kuwait City, enrich the taxi drivers with large-denomination dollar bills, rush north to the American tank park near the power station, interview all available princes and politicians, peer across the border berms and earthworks, watch reconnaissance units manoeuvring for a war that would never materialize, and then, when it didn't, head home laden with souvenirs from the hospitable Sheraton Hotel. It wasn't really journalism at all, but an original way of keeping the peace by pretending to go to war. It was the moment when news grew stale for me and lost its novelty. I realized that after thirty years on the road I was doing no more than going through the motions, and if I ever got a chance of a second career, I should jump at it – which, in due course, I did.

The CNN Effect

We live at a point of intersection between warfare and news, in which for the first time in history the means of mass destruction have coincided with the means of mass communication. The results of a targeting error or a costly ground offensive will be flashed around the world, unless prevented by censorship, on the day that it occurs; and even censorship won't hold back the tide of bad news for more than a few days. Television is no more morally neutral than the people who control it. It is an instrument, just as an axe is an instrument. And just as an axe can equally be used for forestry or murder, so the camera is also a force for good or evil – for revealing the truth or distorting it, for increasing understanding or inflaming hatred, according to who possesses it, and for what purposes it is used.

How Goebbels would have loved it! How he would have exploited it, and how creatively he would have used it to bewitch the nation, as he did with film and radio! Television works its most powerful magic with swirling images and soaring sound-tracks playing to each others' strengths in a packed and colourful arena. Imagine what it could have done with the music, the banners and the spectacles of Hitler's Germany, the Nuremberg rallies live as they happened, or *The Triumph of the Will* as a TV series beamed into every home. The medium would have been as potent in defeat as in victory. I am heading into controversial territory here, but it is an interesting speculation whether, had satellite television existed in the 1940s, the fire-bombing of Dresden and Hamburg by the British and American air forces would have been politically sustainable, or whether the tens of thousands of civilian casualties and the images beamed up from the smoking ruins would have turned the home front against the prosecution of the war by such ruthless and brutal means. Would people have danced in the streets of London and Coventry in the belief that the Germans had it coming to them? Or would they have been appalled even in those shattered cities by what they saw, and concluded that the carpet-bombing of centres of population was an unacceptable strategy of fighting evil with evil? Even without the hindsight of history, Churchill wrote to the Chiefs of Staff: 'We shall come into control of an utterly ruined land ... The destruction of Dresden remains a serious query against the conduct of Allied bombing.'[3]

The same considerations would have applied to Allied casualties. Today's risk-averse and media-aware commanders are expected to conduct campaigns that not only deliver victory, but do so on a smooth trajectory without setbacks or serious casualties. That is historically an impossible requirement, since wars tend not to come in those shapes and sizes; and it doesn't allow for the human factor, the foul-ups and SNAFUs which are unavoidable in the heat of battle, whatever the balance of forces. It is doubtful whether, under the remorseless spotlight of today's rolling news machines, or the day-to-day carping and conjecture-mongering of their commentators, public opinion would have accepted the costs of the Normandy landings in 1944 as a price worth paying for victory. Further back still, could the sacrificial strategies of the Battle of the Somme in July 1916 even have been contemplated? They would be unthinkable today. The defeat of the twelve divisions of General Gough's Fifth Army on the same front in March 1918 would have been regarded, under the deafening drumbeat of rolling news, as the prelude to total disaster; and the commander himself would have been subjected to a fearsome roasting under the media grill: 'So, General, what went wrong? ... Shouldn't you have predicted the German offensive? ... How many men and guns have you lost? ... How many ammunition depots have been overrun? ... Why did you reorganize your brigades on the eve of the battle so that they hardly knew each other? ... Do you agree with the respected commentator Mr Rudyard Kipling that it was a collapse such as has never befallen British arms in the history of her people?'[4] Television is a fretful medium at the best of times, with a bias towards the bad news over the good, and an unparalleled capacity at the worst of times for spreading defeatism and panic.

In the 1990s much ink was spilled in media journals on the so-called CNN effect – the tendency of governments to adjust their policies to cope with the something-must-be-done demands generated by TV coverage of a humanitarian crisis. This especially applied to Somalia, Rwanda and Bosnia where the Western democracies essentially had no policies, but policy vacuums waiting to be filled. In Somalia, it was the media that got the United States into it and then, gravely damaged on CNN, out of it. Rwanda was an opportunity to save lives that, for reasons of international cowardice, was never taken: there was a lingering suspicion of racism in the decision-making. In Bosnia, belated and remedial actions were taken which, without television, would not even have been considered; and those of us who were accused of being members of the something-must-be-done club, by the then Foreign Secretary Douglas Hurd, among others, have no need to apologize. With respect, we stayed there in circumstances from which others fled, and we tried to help as well as to report.

That phase has passed. In the early twenty-first century the *real* CNN effect is a phenomenon of the battlefield. It can take two forms, and involves either the exploitation or obstruction of the media. One option is that, in a just and popular cause, television should be embedded with the military, and report the war as no war has ever been reported since the arrival of mass media on the scene. This was the innovative model for the Second Gulf War. It introduced a new word to the debate, the 'embeds' – correspondents embedded for the duration of the war into a military unit. It enabled some of the best and worst

37

of war reporting – truth and hype in variable proportions, just as reporters themselves can be truthful or vainglorious according to no known formula. I shall return to these issues in chapter 12.

The alternative doctrine, applied in Afghanistan, is that military operations should be conducted, as far as possible, by surrogates and out of the cameras' range. This new way of waging war takes a variety of forms: an emphasis on remote, unmanned and stand-off weapons systems such as drones and missiles, the extensive use of special forces and covert operations, and the financing and recruitment of rebel groups to destabilize the target regime and liberate the country indigenously. Where the Americans are involved, their foot soldiers in this world of secret warfare will not be massed infantry or armoured formations of the kind that the press can find, film and report on, but small groups of more elusive and shadowy figures: special forces, secret soldiers, military advisers, forward air controllers, intelligence agents, interrogators and CIA paymasters armed with cubic metres of cash. We are reliably informed that American operations in Afghanistan in November 2001 were funded by an agent code-named Gary, whose weapon of war was a strapped metal suitcase containing $3 million in non-sequential $100 bills: 'He always laughed when he saw a television show or movie where someone passed $1 million in a small attaché case. It just wouldn't fit.'[5]

This is a long way from the storm-that-hill traditions of the US military, representing a change of culture as well as of practice. This new kind of warfare is light years away from the old one. The United States is an imperial power – no other description does it justice; but from the halls of Montezuma to the shores of Tripoli it sometimes prefers to do its business deniably, at a distance and by stealth. The country which more than any other has stood for a free press, an open society and an accountable democratic process, has had second thoughts about how much press freedom is too much – which is *all* press freedom in and around those wars that it decides to wage in secret. There may be open coverage of its pre-war live-fire exercises, and briefings and press conferences after the event, but its agents in the field when the real thing happens will prowl unseen like creatures of the night.

The development of the new doctrine has been revealingly set out by Bob Woodward, the Washington journalist who was the scourge of one Republican president, Richard Nixon, in 1972, and then thirty years later the mouthpiece and apologist for another. For his book *Bush at War* he was granted privileged access to all the main players, President George W. Bush and his inner circle, in their decision-making on Afghanistan and Iraq following the attacks on New York and Washington on 11 September 2001. It is a disturbing dossier – at least as alarming, although probably unintentionally, as Mr Woodward's co-authored account of the abuse of presidential power in *All The President's Men*. President Bush comes over as a gunslinger on an unfamiliar range ('Go get the guns! Get my horses! – all the Texas, Alamo macho that made Powell uncomfortable'[6]), and an angry man in charge of an angry nation – a nation demanding vengeance against someone somewhere sometime soon, starting in the enemy's lair in Afghanistan: 'Full force of the US military,' he told Tony Blair in the White House, and 'bombers coming from all directions'.[7] In his speech to Congress that night, seen by a television audience of 80 million, he prepared them for a different kind of war: 'Americans should not expect one battle but a lengthy campaign, unlike any other we have ever seen. It may include dramatic strikes visible on TV, and covert operations, secret even in success.'[8] Even bomb-damage assessments, which had been routinely placed into the public domain from Vietnam to Kosovo, would now be held within the walls of the Pentagon: 'The BDA was going to be treated as highly classified and the press and public would not be told much.'[9] And Secretary of State Colin Powell warned his colleagues to stay away from CNN, because instantaneous battlefield coverage would create unnecessary pressures. 'The biggest problem we have,' said Bush, 'is an impatient press corps. They want the war over yesterday. They don't get it.'[10] His anxieties were misplaced. The American press, in the aftermath of 11 September, was totally at one with the White House and raised no outcry against the new restrictions. If you were looking for impartial, enquiring journalism, the land of the free and home of the brave was not the place to find it.

The Americans even added a further refinement new to the practice of warfare: the inclusion of TV stations on the list of legitimate military targets. In an oblique salute to the power and reach of television, the Pentagon decided that if it couldn't be controlled, the next best thing was to bomb it. That was the fate of the al-Jazeera office in Kabul, blown to bits by American rockets in November 2001, as it had been of Belgrade television in May 1999, and Baghdad television in March 2003. From the American media, guardians of the First Amendment and freedom of the press, there came not a whisper of protest. The great American tradition of telling truth to power was incinerated in New York on 11 September 2001. One of its last defenders, Norman Mailer, observed: 'Democracy is vulnerable ... we will do well to find the rampart we can stand on over what may be the dire years to come.'[11]

3

War, Lies and Videotape

The Nineteenth Century

I am not a wealthy man, except in the books inherited from my father and grandfather. They include a signed edition of *Undertones of War*, by Edmund Blunden, one of the remarkable generation of soldier poets whose accounts of the sacrificial strategies of the Great War changed our attitudes to warfare for ever. No future British commander – Montgomery was an example, even at Arnhem – would be so reckless with his soldiers' lives. The book is dedicated to my father, who was his friend in Suffolk after the war was over: 'Adrian Bell having licensed Edmund Blunden wantonly to disfigure this book deserves all he gets, and may E.B. say that, while no Gainsborough, he yet took a prize for drawing at Yalding Boys' School in 1902, which should at least be more than the late D. H. Lawrence has done.' The disfigurement takes the form of two maps, finely drawn in ink with a thin nib and a rare sense of perspective, of the battlefield near Thiepval south of the River Ancre where the 11th Royal Sussex, Blunden's battalion, lost half its men in an ill-fated attack on the German front lines in November 1916. They went over the top with four companies and came back with two: 'Yet, still, they were a capable battalion, deserving far better treatment than they were now getting, and a battle, not a massacre.'[1] How few of us have faced death every day? How few of us can understand, nearly a century later, what it was like for the soldiers to know, when the sun rose over the German lines, how much the less were their chances of seeing it set behind their own? Blunden survived two years of front-line duty, which was rare at the time. Shortly before leaving Flanders, he attended a lecture by a war correspondent in a rest area, 'who invited questions, whereon a swarthy old colonel rose and said, "The other day I was obliged to take part in a battle. I afterwards read a war correspondent's account of the battle, which proved to me that I hadn't been there at all. Will the lecturer explain that, please?"'[2]

In the century and a half during which war reporters have plied their trade, the media and military have fought their own war of attrition across a contested frontier. The reporters have tried everything from abject surrender to open defiance. The soldiers have counter-attacked with everything from total secrecy and denial of access to (more recently) 'embedding' journalists with military formations in time of war. Are they anywhere near achieving a *modus vivendi*? It is important that they should. Our soldiers defend us and our reporters inform us. They are different sorts of people, but they serve the same society. When an army goes to war in a popularly supported cause, there is no reason why they should be eternally at each others' throats. Both in war fighting and peacekeeping, it is better that they should not be.

The founding father of the trade, first civilian war correspondent and 'miserable parent of a luckless tribe', was William Howard Russell of *The Times*, who was assigned to the Crimean War, with letters of accreditation, in 1854. He walked into an ill-provided and ill-led campaign, and asked his editor, John Delane, 'Am I to tell these things, or hold my tongue?' It is the war reporter's question to this day. The renowned British Army, rivalled only by the German and Israeli Armies as the world's most successful, has been at its least effective when going to war after a long period of peacetime soldiering. Some of the commanders need to be replaced in short order; and if they are not, the results can be catastrophic. So it was in the Crimean War. Russell was not thanked by the generals for exposing the shortcomings of an ill-prepared expedition. He was cast out to the fringes of the battlefield and earned the distinction of being the first reporter subjected to military censorship. He even had his tent cut down. Such harassments belong to the natural order of things. They have continued across the years in many ways and many war zones. They are with us to this day. Having a tent cut down is a harmless reprisal compared to being targeted by an air force which believes that a satellite transmission dish represents 'significant military activity' and sees nothing wrong in destroying TV stations and transmitters. That is how far we have come in the century and a half of war reporting since William Russell. The BBC's Nik Gowing notes with alarm: 'We are being actively targeted by warriors, warlords and even the most highly developed governments, who do not want us to see what they are doing.'[3]

I know of no reporter worth his salt who has not at some time had a stand-up row with a general, and no general who has not reciprocated. There is no harm in that. They have no more right to command us than we have a duty to obey them. I used to lecture at the Army Staff College in Camberley when there still was one. The cut and thrust was vigorous. The soldier's instinct is to censor and be safe, and the journalist's to publish and be damned. Yet in the twenty-first century, as I have mentioned, they both reflect and serve the same community. The difference today is that, thanks to more than fifty years without a global conflict and forty without conscription, we are almost all civilians. We depend for our front-line reporting on a generation of war reporters who, like the politicians, lack personal experience of soldiering. With the distinguished exception of the unkempt Anthony Loyd of *The Times*, who does not look at all like the Royal Green Jackets captain he used to be, they have never worn the uniform, held a rifle, dismantled a machine gun or suffered the close attentions of a sergeant major. In individual cases this may not matter. One of the most successful

British correspondents in the Second Gulf War – assigned to the US Marine Corps almost by accident – was David Willis, the BBC's show-business correspondent from Los Angeles, who never met a cliché he didn't like. (Or maybe it wasn't such a fluke: some of the war coverage across many fronts was so spectacular that it had an unnerving Hollywood quality to it – not so much news as 'militainment'.) But in general soldiers would rather work with reporters who know the difference between a brigade and a battalion, a tank and an armoured personnel carrier, a brigadier and a bombardier.

Man is the most aggressive and destructive animal on the planet. His nature is unlikely to change. It is safe to assume that wars, like death and taxes, will always be with us. British armed forces remain on active service – peacekeeping, peace enforcing and more recently war fighting – in many parts of the world. Very seldom does a year pass but that some of them will have lost their lives in the course of duty. Those losses are not negligible. They were the highest in Iraq in 2003 since the Falkland Islands in 1982. It was harder for the families to bear them because they were suffered in a discretionary war – a war to which there was a diplomatic alternative, before Washington's patience ran out; and too many of the casualties were inflicted by 'friendly fire'. In my one and only appearance in the pulpit of the Guards' Chapel, at a Christmas carol service while I was still an MP, I described those who follow the profession of arms as standing upon the ramparts of our freedom. I threw in some remarks about the duty of care, which were aimed at the top brass and the politicians. The duty of care includes not sending the armed forces to war except in the most extreme and unavoidable circumstances. Their tradition of service and sacrifice is too much taken for granted. They continue to stand upon the ramparts of our freedom – so long as they are not politically misdirected, which it is the business of democracy to prevent. By this I mean real democracy, which does not sanction going to war on a prime minister's whim or a superpower's coat-tails.

If the cause is unjust, the antagonism between the military and the media is necessary; if just, it is a total waste of energy. We are in this together. The time is right for a new understanding – a *settlement*, in the modern idiom – between those who defend us and those who inform us. Such a settlement was attempted in the Second Gulf War of 2003. I shall assess the pluses and minuses of embedded journalism in chapter 12.

The old way of doing things was the naval way. The Senior Service was also the silent service.

Nelson's navy did well enough at Trafalgar without a tumult of scribblers hanging around the fleet. 'The Navy is very old and very wise,' wrote Rudyard Kipling. The press gang had another meaning in those days; and the theory of press relations was that the Navy would sail over the horizon, do its business, and return to proclaim its victory to a grateful nation. Nelson was lionized like no serving officer before or since. He was the most admired man in the kingdom. Like many others, he cared for the publicity but not for the press.

The Twentieth Century

In the Second World War, wrote the historian Philip Knightley, 'The Royal Navy, true to its First World War form, decided that it had no room on its ships for correspondents and would see the war through without them.'[4] Something of the same kind was proposed as recently as 1982, when the Navy was the lead service and the British Task Force was being assembled to recapture the Falkland Islands from Argentina's occupation. The plan was modified by the Prime Minister, Margaret Thatcher, who had a more modern idea of communications and insisted on the presence of a small pool of press to accompany the armed forces. It was a bruising experience for all of them, in the direct Crimean tradition. I was marooned in the BBC's Washington bureau at the time, and disappointed not to be sailing into battle with the rest of them, but from the later reports I realize now that it was a very good war to miss. The hostilities between the press pool and its Ministry of Defence minders were matched by those between the reporters themselves. Journalists, then as now, were their own worst enemies.

It wasn't just a pool: it was a piranha pond. There were two of its members, in my view, who came out of it with special credit. One was Brian Hanrahan, the BBC man nearest the door when the Falkland Islands were invaded; he was a newcomer to the reporting staff on attachment from the photographic library at the TV centre; he was sensible and resourceful and had a way with words; he launched his career with a single censorship-friendly line about the Harrier jets on the aircraft carrier – 'I counted them all out and I counted them all back' – which belonged to the category of phrases we all wish we'd thought of. It made a great impact at the time and led to others trying to emulate him for years to come. The unsung hero of the hour was Brian's cameraman, Bernard Hesketh, a BBC veteran who was well on the downhill side of fifty-five when he was assigned to the Falklands War.

It was no easy victory, but a close-run thing. The searing pictures of burning ships and wounded soldiers at Bluff Cove were his. It was the government's good fortune that, because of the antique communication system, they were not transmitted until after the victory. I had worked with Bernard and liked him from Vietnam to Beirut and Angola; but that's inadequate: you don't *like* in those circumstances – you *love*. Towards the end of my career I only went to war with people I loved. Bernard had an unnerving habit of filming a fire-fight – a real battle with real bullets flying around – with a camera set on an old-fashioned surveyor's tripod, when anyone sensible would have held it on his shoulder, or thrown it away and looked for a hole to hide in. Bernard needed a personal bodyguard and security adviser to keep him out of trouble. The BBC in those days didn't employ such people, so I did my best. I urged his loyal soundman and subaltern, Barry Lanchester, to head for the nearest ditch and stay there until the battle was over.

Bernard was courageous beyond the call of duty. He was also an English gentleman through and through, in the truest meaning of the term, which is defined not by class but by character. He was unimpressed when, on the voyage to the South Atlantic, a young officer, so far untested in combat, dared to question his patriotism on the spurious grounds that he came from the tribe of journalists. Bernard rolled up his trouser leg and showed the shrapnel wounds he had received on board a Royal Navy ship in 1944. 'Young man,' he said quietly, 'I think you should know that I got those on active service against the Germans some years before you were born.' The officer fell silent. Steadiness under fire is not a quality that comes automatically with the Queen's commission. You don't know how you will react until the incoming rounds part the air above your head or ricochet off the wall behind you. At that point you live your life one second at a time; and you are grateful for every shot you hear, because if you can hear it, it hasn't killed you.

Then there was the Max Hastings phenomenon. Max was a would-be soldier who had once been an officer cadet with the Parachute Regiment, until they parted by mutual agreement, because of his Maxocentric character and lack of the team spirit that goes with soldiering; but he looked and sounded officer class, and of all the press gang on the Falklands he had the best contacts with the military, which he was able to exploit to his tactical advantage, especially in hitching rides on helicopters. This put him not only with the troops advancing into Port Stanley, but actually ahead of them at the climax of the campaign. 'Max Hastings leads the way,' boasted the *Evening Standard* under its full-page headline, 'First Man Into Stanley'.

It was a real scoop but a controversial one. The record shows that reporters who liberate places attract the wrath and envy of their colleagues. Max's rivals caught up with him at the surrender, and on his way back to the ship to file his copy he was entrusted with their stories as well as his own. Journalists trust each other only when they have to. What was never adequately explained was how it was that his was the only report to reach a London news desk in time to be used. His rivals' sense of grievance persisted over the years, and did not diminish with the editorships and the knighthood that accrued to him. They saw him as definitely not one of them, but an aspiring grandee or (in his words) a 'stuck-up middle-class woofter'. In his memoir *Going to the Wars*, a book so self-revealing that if anyone else had written it about him he should have sued, he told the story of one of his colleagues who had had to be dissuaded by another from running him through with a bayonet. The man from the *Yorkshire Post* observed regretfully: 'This is neither the time nor the place to kill Max Hastings.'

It was in no one's interests, when next the British went to war, to repeat the anarchic Falklands experience of a press corps at war with its minders and itself. In a series of consultations across the no-man's-land of media–military relations – the press on one side and the Ministry of Defence on the other – a serious attempt was made to learn and apply the lessons of the South Atlantic. The result was a more structured, better resourced and collaborative scheme of telling the soldiers' story when the British did next go to war, which was in the Gulf after the Iraqi invasion of Kuwait in 1990. It consisted of a small press pool alongside each of the armoured brigades, the 4th and the 7th, and another at Divisional Headquarters, where Kate Adie was the voice of authority and all-purpose warrior queen. Even those of us who had once been soldiers had a lot to learn about the rules of engagement and the new way of going to war. Early in the exercise Kate questioned an order from one of her minders, Lieutenant Colonel (now Brigadier) Chris Sexton of the Royal Engineers. 'Kate,' he said, 'the question "why?" is not an army question.' This was the beginning of embedded journalism. She described the status we occupied as 'somewhere between a completely useless recruit and a very dim officer'.[5] I have a modest claim to notoriety as the first embedded war reporter. My papers include an accreditation card, serial number 001, which describes itself as 'Authority for a British War Correspondent to Accompany an Operational Force'.

The theory was not put as fully into practice as it was in the Second Gulf War; but the principle was the same: that the soldiers and journalists should operate alongside each other. To my relief, the liberator of Port Stanley was no longer part of the battle order: the business of reporting a war was already hard enough without being scooped by Max Hastings. Such unlikely bedfellows as Reuters, the BBC, *The Times* and *The People* were thrust into uniform and posted to a remote corner of Saudi Arabia with the Desert Rats, the 7th Armoured Brigade. We camped in a circle with the Ordnance Corps, the Intelligence Corps, the signallers, the mail tent and the cooks. They had been forbidden to use the term 'Remfs' on their radios, which meant a rear echelon something-or-other. So they invented Pontis – Persons Of No Tactical Importance. We definitely belonged in the category of Pontis.

Like the embedded correspondents of the Second Gulf War, we made a kind of Faustian pact with our minders, exchanging access for freedom. The difference was that in our case it didn't amount to very much more than a what-might-have-been. The war itself was a slight affair, as most of the Iraqi resistance crumbled without a shot being fired. Our coverage of it, the tanks of the Queen's Royal Irish Hussars charging across the Iraqi border to the Basra Road, was vivid and authentic all right, but lost in the desert. The technology was not as advanced as we needed, and as it became twelve years later, when a tank could as well be a platform for a gyro-stabilized satellite dish as for a gun. Our transmission system was adrift in a convoy many miles behind us and the outcome joined the immense back catalogue of forgettable television.

The Twenty-First Century

I was lucky that by the dawn of the new millennium I had moved from the war zones to the lesser conflicts of the House of Commons. The wars of the twenty-first century were initially marked by a return to the suspicions and secrecy of the past. It was as if the lessons of the Falklands and the Gulf had never been learned. The Royal Marines' operations in Afghanistan in 2002 were a model of how not to manage relations between the media and the military. It is a truth of warfare, universally acknowledged, that no plan remains intact after its first contact with reality. Gung-ho announcements of the expedition's object-ives were bound to lead to anticlimax when the enemy mys-teriously melted away into the mountains and not a shot was fired in anger. The moral of this is that when first you arrive in a war zone it is wise to stay silent, or at least laconic, since by the time you have deployed the situation will have changed beyond recognition. Nor is it sensible to confine the press to a fly-blown encampment on an airfield and give them access only to briefings and occasional stage-managed field trips. What they don't see they won't believe.

The losers were not only the press but the Royal Marines. Their real achievements, in finding and destroying arms dumps and denying the Taleban fighters their mountain hideouts, were never properly acknowledged. Nor was the role of the 1st Battalion the Royal Anglian Regiment, heirs and successors to the steady traditions of the Suffolk Regiment, in keeping the peace in Kabul. Journalists are a capricious, self-serving lot and perhaps not as good at neutrality as they think they are. They are either with you or against you. They tend to look for what they want to find – and then to find what they're looking for. A point that I made time and time again to soldiers in their academies and study days was not to be too nervous about it. A good battalion will not be troubled by a hostile headline, which everyone but the Defence Secretary's anxiety brigade will have forgotten by tomorrow. Better to seize the moment and take the initiative. Soldiers are taught to get inside an enemy's decision-making loop. It applies just as much to their traffic with the media.

A field commander's most important constituency, in dealing with the press in time of war, is the families of the soldiers serving under him. If he is wise he will advise them not to aggravate their anxieties by paying a moment's attention to the rumour bazaar of twenty-four-hour TV news; but he also has an opportunity to communicate with them that was never available to his predecessors (or in the case of the Boer and Crimean campaigns even desirable – it would be hard to imagine the patrician Lord Raglan on the end of a satellite uplink). Adverse coverage will not immediately affect the men in the front line – they will not know of it till later – but it will demoralize their families at home and undermine wider support for the campaign in which their lives are on the line. Confident and straightforward press relations require the maximum access consistent with operational security. This will involve some calculated risk-taking, but will bring its rewards both on and off the battlefield. It should apply to all units except special forces, and I am no longer sure about the special forces. Until now they have operated under separate rules, because of the secrecy that is part of their mystique but that they themselves have compromised. The men from Hereford have increasingly tended to pick up their lap-tops when they laid down their Uzi sub-machine guns. The result has been a spate of SAS books, which have made the names of a few individuals but caused much grief in the Regiment. The secret soldiers also fight in our name. As their role expands, we have a right to know more about them.

There is one other indispensable element: the democratic legitimacy of the military operations undertaken in our name. In today's less deferential world, the sacrifices of Edmund Blunden's generation and the 11th Royal Sussex are no longer supportable, if for no other reason than that they would not play well on Sky News. The forces that nominally serve the Crown actually serve the people. Indeed, as the greatest Independent MP, William Cobbett, observed, they are the people under arms and always have been. Battles are not won by officers alone and are sometimes won in spite of them. The war memorials on every village green in the country bear granite witness to the tradition of sacrifice by all the people, of whom the rank and file are by far the more numerous, and to the fates of regiments that deserved a battle not a massacre. Public support for the troops' deployment in any cause is vital. Without it the enterprise will fail, as at Suez in 1956. The Falklands campaign in 1982 had that support, as did the First Gulf War in 1991. The Second Gulf War of 2003 was an altogether more questionable adventure. When the Spanish Prime Minister, Jose Maria Aznar, confessed that only 4 per cent of his people supported it, Tony Blair told him, according to an interview in the *Sun*, 'Crikey – that's even less than the number who think Elvis Presley is alive.' ('Crikey' translates into Spanish, approximately, as *caramba*!)

War reporters in the past tended to be viewed by field commanders as something of a nuisance, but – rather like the weather – a nuisance to be endured and dealt with. The way of proceeding was to try to get them, as the saying was, 'onside' – and, if they were not onside, to censor or exclude them. Then they were peripheral to the conduct of the war: now they are central to it. To influence opinion at home and abroad, and even in the theatre of war itself, governments wage a total information campaign and armies conduct information operations planned in detail. These include PSYOPs (psychological operations, including broadcasts and leaflet drops aimed at enemy soldiers and civilians), deception measures and relations with the press. The first shipment of aid to reach Iraq while the war of 2003 was still being fought included food, water, medicine – and a satellite TV ground station. In an age of multi-channel television beamed across borders, the broadcasters, whether they like it or not, are main players in the information campaign.

In the First Gulf War, at a negotiation in a tent in Saudi Arabia, we were promised by the army, in the persons of Colonel John King and Lieutenant Colonel Chris Sexton, that their deception strategy would not include feeding false information to the press. They kept their word. In the Second Gulf War there seems to have been no such guarantee, but a measure of spill-over from deception measures into media briefings. Centcom's 'podium of truth' at its Qatar headquarters was a one-sided platform that emphasized the precision of the new weaponry but was imprecise about the civilian casualties it caused; and the three-week war featured a series of rumours broadcast on Western TV stations which, had they been true, would consistently have advanced the allied cause. These included the early fall of the port of Umm Qasr, the death of Saddam Hussein, the defection of his deputy Tariq Aziz, the discovery of a suspected chemical weapons site, and a popular uprising against the regime in Basra. Not one of these reports was true or verifiable at the time when it was broadcast. Together, they were advertised as breaking news. Rather, they were breaking rumour. They were prominently featured on the satellite channels, especially Murdoch's Sky News. They created a sense of momentum by the British and American forces. It is an old technique, transferred from political to military campaigns, in which the appearance of momentum generates the real thing. It runs in the American first family: George W. Bush's father, when he was campaigning for the presidency in the snows of Iowa, used to call it 'Big Mo'.

In the twenty-first century war reporters will inevitably become targets and conduits for spin and manipulation: the vogue word for it is 'contextualization'. Alastair Campbell complained that 'sometimes events can be reported ... before we are in a position to contextualize and give comments upon them.' How very unreasonable of those events to occur before being contextualized.

In such a situation the reporters behind enemy lines – in Belgrade, Kabul or Baghdad, wherever the enemy of the moment is identified – will inevitably be vilified for giving comfort to an evil regime in an evil axis. What is more worrying is the willingness of some journalists, even today, to do the propagandists' work for them. This is not an entirely new phenomenon. Philip Knightley describes the part played by accredited British correspondents from 1914 to 1918 in a conspiracy to conceal the truth of the Great War:

> They were in a position to know more than most men of the nature of the war of attrition on the Western Front, yet they identified themselves absolutely with the armies in the field; they protected the high command from criticism, wrote jauntily about life in the trenches, kept an inspired silence about the slaughter, and allowed themselves to be used by the propaganda machine.[6]

To the men in the trenches the two least welcome categories of visitors were the staff officers, with their red tabs, and the war correspondents, with their green armbands. The green armbands were held in even lower esteem than the red tabs.

It is generally accepted now that, of the men who wrote contemporary accounts of the war, it was the reporters who told the lies and the poets who told the truths. They were dealt with according to their merits by the powers-that-were. When it was all over, Fleet Street's finest were rewarded with knighthoods and their newspaper owners with peerages. One of the greatest of the war poets – I would say *the* greatest (I used to take his poems to the wars) – was Wilfred Owen of the 2ND Manchesters. His reward was to be hospitalized for shell-shock, and then to be killed crossing a canal in the war's last week. The dead were ignored by the reporters but not by the poets.

> No mockeries now for them; no prayers nor bells,
> Nor any voice of mourning save the choirs, –

The shrill, demented choirs of wailing shells;
And bugles calling for them from sad shires.[7]

Can today's journalists match the partisanship of their predecessors? They can, and some of them do. Not only that, but
they go even further than the gentleman correspondents of the
Great War in urging the military to conduct its campaigns even
more ruthlessly than it would have done without them. This
applies especially to the Americans. An example is the TV
station in Baghdad which, in March 2003, was alleged to be
spewing out lies and propaganda and making it harder for the
Americans to wage their war of liberation. Here is a cross-
section of statements about it from influential reporters and
commentators on the mainstream American networks: 'To the
surprise of many, the US has not taken out Iraq's TV headquarters' (NBC); 'A lot of people wondered why Iraqi TV had
been allowed to stay on the air' (CNN); 'Should we take Iraqi
TV off the air? Should we put one down the stovepipe
there?'(Fox News). When the station was bombed on 25 March,
one of the commentators boasted that 'criticism about allowing
Saddam Hussein to talk to his citizens and lie to them had had
an effect'.[8]

A TV station is a civilian installation. Attacks on civilian
targets are clearly and explicitly forbidden under the Geneva
Conventions. Yet here we had American journalists, some of
them highly respected names in the TV establishment, encouraging the allied forces to take actions which, however precisely
conducted, would kill civilians, including fellow journalists.
This suggests a number of circumstances discomforting to those
who believe in open, honest and enquiring journalism: the ruth-
lessness and pervasiveness of the total information war, the
willingness of high-profile journalists to follow the flag at whatever cost to their principles; the abdication by the TV networks
of their role of independent witness and scrutiny. The war in
Iraq was not their finest hour.

I have long argued for a committed and even impassioned journalism, as careful of the truth as of the consequences of what it writes and shows. That is the opposite of a journalism under arms, marching to war in lock-step with the military, credulous of the claims of the high command and even proposing new and wider bombing targets. The Islamic storm-troopers who brought down the Twin Towers caused more devastation in the United States than they knew. The collateral damage extended to the American press, which suffered from the shock and fury of the times and has still not recovered the sureness of its footing. It was tested and found wanting. Under pressure, it failed and folded. It lacked the essential front-line quality of steadiness under fire. By contrast the British media, so much further from the epicentre, clung on to the tradition of editorial independence, albeit with some wavering around their foreign-owned fringes. The press offered a healthy diversity of views for and against the war, both between newspapers and within them. The most trenchant arguments against the use of force were made by Matthew Parris in a salvo of four columns in Murdoch's *Times*.

The winners of the war included Fox News (motto 'fair and balanced', proprietor Rupert Murdoch), the self-appointed scourge of the supposedly liberal bias of the media establishment. Fox had a successful war. It outperformed its American rivals in its front line coverage, in its ratings and in its flag-waving for the war effort; although in the flag-waving department the rest weren't far behind. Seen in this light, the attack on the Baghdad TV station had a certain logic to it. In the new, bleak and lawless landscape of armed conflict, TV does indeed have military purposes. It manages perceptions and shapes the battlefield. Wars can be won by television as well as by precision-guided missiles. Indeed they cannot be won *without* television. The missiles alone will not deliver victory. To win a war, you have in the first phase to be *seen* to be winning it: that was the effect of the spate of dubious rumours given credence on the twenty-four-hour news channels. Then, in the last phase, you have to be *seen* to have won it: that also is for the cameras to deliver.

There is a technique in television known as the 'as live'. It is a broadcast that seems to be live, but is in fact pre-recorded – a relatively mild and harmless deception compared to some of the others practised by a medium that can lie like a trooper when so minded. Thanks to the Second Gulf War, there is now a matching technique in warfare known as the 'as dead'. It applied to Saddam Hussein's removal from power. Whether he had fled the country or been blown away by a 2,000 pound bomb seemed in the end to be of little consequence. He was yesterday's tyrant. He was functionally 'as dead'. It was television that partly procured and entirely proclaimed his downfall. The image of a toppled statue defined the moment of victory.

4

Living with Terrorism

Old Terrorism

The attacks on the World Trade Center and the Pentagon on 11 September 2001 were not only the most lethal acts of terrorism ever perpetrated; they represented a new kind of terrorism, harder to deal with or guard against, less susceptible to a negotiated conclusion, and closer to warfare in the scale of their death toll than anything that had gone before. They changed our view of the world in which we live. They called into question its survivability. Just as today's famines in Africa are new variant famines, different in character from those of the past, so today's terrorism is new variant terrorism. It has something in common with the SARS epidemic – a new and well-travelled virus that spreads in rapid and mysterious ways, thrives on panic and has so far no known cure.

Terrorism is notoriously as difficult to define as to defeat. It is a term with which governments like to brand their enemies, both internal and external, as outcasts and criminals. An emotionally uncluttered definition of a terrorist is 'someone who uses terror against civilians to achieve a political objective'. This does not exclude state terrorism, of the kind that dictators can inflict on their citizens or empires on their subject peoples. Nor does it include all actions by insurgent forces against the civil power. A bomb in a restaurant or hotel is an act of terrorism; an ambush of an army patrol is not – soldiers can be frightened, but they cannot be terrorized. This seems a reasonable distinction to make, and one that helps resolve the old conundrum about whether one man's terrorist is another man's freedom fighter; or, to take it a stage further, whether terrorism is the war of the weak and war is the terrorism of the strong. I used to dismiss this as a merely polemical conjecture; but the more I see of the world's disorders, the more I suspect that there is a jagged and awkward fragment of truth in it. Certainly the British and Americans could have refuted it more easily, in the aftermath of the Gulf War of 2003, if their precision-guided weapons had not killed and maimed so many innocent people, if they had not used depleted-uranium munitions, which are linked by a growing body of evidence to birth defects and leukaemia among the young, and if they had not included in their arsenal the cluster bombs that they dropped in all recent conflicts – Kosovo, Afghanistan and Iraq – which have the characteristics of aerially sown anti-personnel mines. If the British and Americans are accused of practising state terrorism, their best defence is the distinction between intention and effect. Their intention was to use these weapons only for military purposes, whereas the hijackers who brought down the Twin Towers on 11 September timed their attacks to cause the maximum casualties as well as damage. There *is* a difference; but if you were the parent of a child blown up by a cluster bomb, you would find the difference to be of little comfort.

Old and new terrorism are quite distinct. The old terrorism of the last century, and before that the use of terror as a weapon of war, belonged to an earlier and – dare I say it of something so lethal? – a more innocent age. Was there collateral damage at Agincourt or Waterloo? Probably not, except in the sense of the forage and pillage with which armies in the field sustained themselves. The weapons of shock and awe were not yet invented or even imagined. Terrorism itself, in the sense of terrorizing civilian populations to achieve a political or military objective, is a feature of modern rather than ancient warfare. By the time of the Second World War the technology of terrorism was already work in progress. Both the German and British air forces studied and applied

59

it. They experimented with different types of incendiary munitions, not for use only against military targets. The citizens of Coventry in 1940 and Dresden in 1945 were the victims of bombing campaigns intended to kill and terrorize them. Not all those wounds are healed. In February 1995, on the fiftieth anniversary of the bombing of Dresden, the Royal Air Force could still not bring itself to send a representative to the ceremonies of remembrance attended by both countries' military and religious leaders. A field marshal of the Army was present, but not so much as a flight lieutenant of the Royal Air Force.

More recently, terrorism became the means through which dispossessed people, initially Palestinians but latterly also Kurds, Chechens and others, drew attention to their grievances and statelessness. Its trigger was the Arabs' defeat in the Six Days' War of 1967, and Israel's expansion into newly occupied territories. An historic opportunity for peace was lost. There could have been a settlement; but instead, there were only settlements, and the settler-in-chief was Ariel Sharon, who sowed the wind as Agriculture Minister and reaped the whirlwind as Prime Minister. I reported extensively from Israel in those days, including the wars of 1967 and 1973, and subsequent bloody terrorist attacks in Beit Shean and elsewhere, and debated the issue endlessly with my Israeli friends. They argued that, without settlements, there would be no Israel. I replied that, with settlements, there would be no peace. We were probably both right. There is still an Israel but no peace. Sooner or later, unless the hostilities persist until the crack of doom, there will have to be an exchange of territory, including settlements, for peace. *Actions have consequences.* The Balfour Declaration of 1917, of the right of the Jewish people to a homeland in Palestine, was one of the most consequential pieces of paper ever signed.

Terrorism was sponsored by states, which exploited it to fight proxy wars, usually against Israel, and which gave safe haven to the terrorists. Its reach was not global then, but regional. It was real-world, real-time theatre of a kind never seen before –

a stage-managed presentation of murder, hijacking and hostage-taking, played out under the eye of the world's media from the Munich Olympics to the airports and capitals of Europe and the Middle East. The murder of eleven Israeli athletes by Black September terrorists at Munich in 1972 was a brutal episode, but exceptional. The old terrorism was generally marked by a high degree of drama and a low level of casualties.

Smaller European countries proved especially vulnerable. Austria was a favourite target. The first attack was in 1973, when a group of Palestinians abducted three Russian Jews emigrating to Israel, and held them at gunpoint for sixteen hours in Vienna airport, demanding an end to Jewish migration and safe passage out of the country. The Austrian Chancellor, Bruno Kreisky (who was himself Jewish), capitulated. An Austrian official ran across the tarmac to the van where the hijackers were holding their hostages. He handed them a radio set. Vienna's third radio network faded its music programme and Chancellor Kreisky broadcast his promise to close the country's transit facilities for refugees. In immediate terms it was a kind of deliverance. The lives of the hostages were saved. Not a drop of blood was spilt. The hijackers flew out to a heroes' welcome in Tripoli. I reported at the time, 'The likely cost of defying the hijackers is known: it is the lives of *these* three Jewish émigrés and *that* Austrian customs man, threatened by an Arab with a hand-grenade pin between his teeth, out there now on the airport apron, as the final ultimatum expires ... the likely cost of appeasing the hijackers is not known, but it will probably be to encourage and promote further attacks at some other time and some other place.'

I was right about some other time, but wrong about some other place. The terrorists returned to Vienna two years later, and again the Austrians capitulated. This time the hijackers were from the Popular Front for the Liberation of Palestine. They kidnapped eleven oil ministers at the OPEC headquarters, killing an Austrian police officer and two diplomats. The ministers were flown to Algeria and ransomed for a sum of between $20 million and $50 million. Terrorism thus became a supra-national and lucrative business. The ringleader of the raid, and chief racketeer for more than twenty years, was the Venezuelan revolutionary Ilich Ramirez Sanchez, also known as Carlos the Jackal. He was the archetypal figure of the old terrorism, calculating his risks and choosing his targets to deliver the maximum dividends in terms of both profit and publicity. He claimed the moral responsibility for all the PFLP's murders. Having been ousted from the organization for failing to kill the Saudi Arabian and Iranian oil ministers in the OPEC hijack, he founded his own freelance outfit, the Organization for Arab Armed Struggle, to further the cause. He was a busy man, implicated in many bomb blasts in France, an attempted assassination in London and the hijacking of a French airliner to Entebbe in 1976. He may also have had links with Japanese terrorists, Italy's Red Brigades and Germany's Red Army Faction. He killed two French counter-intelligence agents and his Palestinian contact, Michel Moukharbal, when they knocked on his door in Paris in 1975. Not until 1994 did the French catch up with him, when they found out where he was, did a deal with the Sudanese, counter-kidnapped him in Khartoum and flew him home to face trial in Paris. The unrepentant Carlos told the court in 1997, 'When one wages war for thirty years, there is a lot of blood spilled – mine and others. But we never killed anyone for money, but for a cause, the liberation of Palestine.' He was wrong about spilling his own blood – it was the blood of others that he spilled – as many as eighty-three of them. He stayed ahead of a dangerous game until his luck ran out. He is now serving a life sentence for murder.

New Terrorism

The new terrorism would have no place for survivors and opportunists like Carlos the Jackal. It is revolutionary, sectarian, stateless, punitive, extremely violent and as willing to sacrifice the lives of its own people as those of its victims. Those who accuse it of cowardice misuse the language: it is murderous, but not cowardly. Its foot soldiers are suicide bombers seeking martyrdom. Its intention is to purge Islam of Western influences and to establish theocratic states in place of the secular monarchies of the Arab world. Its mission is also to punish and to destroy. It is more lethal than the old terrorism, more implacable, more cellular and less hierarchical in its structure, harder to penetrate and with a wider range of targets across the world – from soft targets like hotels and restaurants, to hard targets like military compounds, and to symbolic targets like the Pentagon and the World Trade Center. Osama bin Laden's response to the events of 11 September 2001 was delayed until four weeks later. It stopped short of claiming direct responsibility for the attacks, but was illuminating about the organization's mind-set and objectives: 'Here is America struck by Allah Almighty in one of its vital organs, so that its greatest buildings are destroyed. Grace and gratitude to Allah ... I swear by Allah that the Americans will never be able to enjoy peace until we live it in Palestine, and before the army of infidels departs the land of Mohammed, peace be upon him.'[1]

The most authoritative account of the mission's planning and execution was provided by my friend Yosri Fouda, chief investigative reporter of al-Jazeera Television. His book *The Masterminds of Terror*, co-authored with Nick Fielding and published in 2003, is required reading for anyone who seeks to understand this unique scourge of our times. For forty-eight hours in Karachi, in April 2002, he stayed with, prayed with and interviewed Khalid Sheikh Mohammed, the head of al-Qaeda's military committee, and Ramzi Binalshibh, coordinator of the 'Holy Tuesday' operation. They wished to mark the first anniversary of the attacks by justifying what they had planned, and by taking credit for it. 'They say that you are terrorists,' Fouda suggested by way of an opening gambit. Ramzi Binal-

63

shibh replied, 'If terrorism is to throw terror into the heart of your enemy and the enemy of Allah, then we thank him, the most Merciful, the most Compassionate, for enabling us to be terrorists.'[2] The interviews were broadcast in September 2002. In circumstances that had nothing to do with the interview, both men were subsequently arrested. Khalid Sheikh Mohammed was sentenced to death for the murder of the American journalist Daniel Pearl.

Two special insights emerge from Yosri Fouda's interviews. One is that Khalid, a man of high intelligence with a relatively affluent background and a privileged British education, was radicalized by his experience of the Bosnian war, when as a nineteen-year-old he sought (unsuccessfully) to join a Muslim militia unit fighting alongside Bosnian government forces. *Actions have consequences.* I claim no gifts of prophecy, but I did describe the Bosnian war, even while it was raging, as the most consequential conflict of our time; and so it proved. Khalid Sheikh Mohammed went on from the Balkans to become a formidable organizer of Islamic fighters elsewhere. He was a master of disguise and surprise, and al-Qaeda's chief of staff. It is at least possible that, if the Western democracies had reacted earlier and more effectively to the blood-letting in Bosnia, the attacks on the World Trade Center and Pentagon nearly ten years later, which were the most complex terrorist operation ever undertaken, might not have occurred at all, or might have failed. Those who believe that the best course of action is inaction are nearly always proved wrong.

The other insight is into al-Qaeda's implacability. This is not an enemy that negotiates: it is an enemy that destroys. Ramzi Binalshibh handed Yosri Fouda a revealing 112-page manifesto seeking to justify the taking of innocent lives on 11 September 2001:

It is agreed that it [America] is a country at war, and a country at war is for Muslims to harm in every way. The blood of its people, their wealth and their women are legitimate targets for Muslims, in the same manner that the Prophet, peace be upon him, did with his foes ... We have seen from the Koran and sunnah that jihad will continue until doomsday ... The fall of 6,333 casualties [a twofold over-estimate] as a result of the 11 September attacks does not heal the breasts of Muslims or bring about their revenge from America. We therefore need a thousand operations like these ...[3]

President Bush's reaction was understandably belligerent: 'They had declared war on us, and I made up my mind at that moment that we were going to war.' To call it a war was one thing, to call it a crusade was another, unwise as well as unhistorical. 'This crusade,' he said, 'this war on terrorism is going to take a while'; and he told Congress: 'I will not relent in waging this struggle for the freedom and security of the American people.'

The problem with using words as weapons of war is that, because they may be interpreted to mean what they say, they ratchet up their own expectations – words of war that will have to be matched by actions, or the warrior king loses credibility. 'War' is the wrong word anyway. Wars have conclusions. They end in victory or defeat, in mutual exhaustion and a negotiated ceasefire, or in a peace imposed by outside powers and alliances. None of these scenarios applies to the 'war' on terrorism, which tempts us to adopt the extremist remedy of answering force with counter-force and terror with counter-terror. This sounds well enough as a soundbite on Fox News, which is exactly why it is so seductive, but it plays into the hands of a ruthless adversary with an intuitive feel for the Western democracies' weaknesses.

Perhaps we are the victims of our fictions – all those disaster movies ending in rescue and deliverance. There is no Rambo or Terminator to come to save the day in the real world of the new terrorism. The celluloid heroes of the big screen, taking fright, are reluctant even to fly to the premieres of their own movies. Instead our post-heroic age offers an imbalance of forces, with

the firepower favouring one side and a fight-to-the-death fanaticism the other. Defeat is unthinkable, but victory unlikely.
We are not dealing here with an enemy who can be overcome
by boots-on-the-ground military force, but with an enemy who
can be contained by patient intelligence work, vigilant policing
and foreign-policy initiatives that have the effect of reducing,
rather than increasing, the flow of volunteers seeking martyrdom in jihad against the West. The war in Iraq did not fall
into that category. What we are engaged on in the long haul is
not a war but a campaign for survival – the survival of our
values as much as ourselves. The values of liberal democracy
are strong, and will prevail – but only in the long term, and if
we don't betray them by our manner of defending them, in the
course of events that will test our deepest reserves of patience
and courage.

I used to give a lecture to military academies entitled (not
very elegantly) 'Shit happens and how to deal with it'. I feel the
same about terrorism. From time to time its agents will penetrate
our defences, especially those of the softer targets, however well
we organize them. That is no reason for us to lead timorous
lives, or to turn our societies inside out and upside down for
fear of what the enemy at the gates may do to us. That gives
him the victory without a shot being fired. Instead, we should
understand that there are no quick fixes or silver bullets available. Terrorism is a fact of twenty-first-century life. We shall
have to learn to take the casualties that it inflicts, to curb it
where we can, and to live with it where we cannot, for many
years to come.

The last things we need are panic and hysteria, complete with
their own delivery system. That, alas, has become the role of
television.

Terrorism and Television

Television is terrorism's medium of choice. It has more immediacy than newspapers, makes more impact than radio. It
reaches across frontiers and shows events live – or almost live –
as they happen. Terrorism seizes opportunities that are now
available on a global scale, and on Arabic as well as Western TV
channels. It delivers unmediated messages through its unwitting
accomplices in the media. It plays to the weakness of television
news, especially of the twenty-four-hour news-on-a-loop variety,
which is the Colosseum of our time: it craves sensation and
confrontation, and needs a constant diet of images of violence
to feed it. TV news is a theatrical medium, and I am grateful to
a friend and former colleague, Vin Ray of the BBC, for publicly
admitting its thespian character: 'Reporting live [is] what actors
sometimes call "being in the moment".'[4] I shall return to his
confessions in chapter 11.

There was no more striking example of the interplay between
the media and the murderer than the hijacking of TWA's Flight
847 by three Lebanese terrorists between Athens and Rome on
14 June 1985. For the next sixteen days the aircraft shuttled
between Beirut and Algiers, releasing passengers, until only
thirty-nine of them, all American men, were left. One of these,
a US Navy diver, was brutally murdered and thrown onto the
tarmac at Beirut Airport. Not only was the TWA flight hijacked
by the incident, so were the TV networks: CBS devoted 68 per
cent of its nightly news broadcasts to it for the duration, NBC
62 per cent and ABC 61 per cent. The wealthiest of advertisers
could not buy that kind of airtime – and the hijackers were
essentially in the advertising business. The rest of the world
stood still for them. Nothing else mattered. In his scholarly
analysis of the event, Professor Gus Martin of California State
University concluded: 'The hijackers masterfully manipulated
the world's media. They granted carefully orchestrated interviews and selected the information they allowed the news outlets

to broadcast . . . They successfully broadcast their grievances and demands to the world and achieved their objectives.'⁵ Americans don't deal well with hostage issues and their emotional fall-out – the tearful special pleading from relatives and the flying of yellow ribbons in front porches in small communities. The Reagan administration, which had come to office on the issue of the storming of the American Embassy in Teheran and a failed attempt to rescue the hostages, put pressure on Israel to release 756 of its Shiite Arab prisoners. The prisoners were released, as were the surviving hostages on the aircraft. The lesson was that terrorism worked, but it didn't work alone. It needed television, just as actors need stages, to give it a platform. This was an early example of the CNN effect even before CNN was fully established as a global force.

Not only is there a synergy between terrorism and television generally: there is an especially close relationship between the new terrorism and new television. They thrive more than ever on attention and spectacle. They prosper more than ever in each other's company. A world without warfare, bombings, hijackings and hostage-takings is not a world in which the rolling news services find it as easy to hold their audiences and justify their existence. They have no such problem in a world where those phenomena are everyday events. The networks' peacetime staples of politics, consumer news, sport, weather, fashion and celebrity profiles will not alone keep their ratings high and their advertisers happy. For that (much more than newspapers) they need sudden and spectacular violence – either the organized violence of warfare or the random violence of crime and terrorism, such as an anthrax-infected letter or a gunman stalking the suburbs of Washington. At that point the news services will go into overdrive and clear their decks of all other programming except the weather forecast. When they are all fired up by a single story, nothing exceeds like excess. Their headlines will proclaim 'SNIPER AT LARGE' for days on end, as if no other news in the world is of any consequence. Their very feverishness abets the gunman by spreading panic though the community and encouraging other, copycat crimes in the future – and this in a country where murder by handgun is endemic, deep-rooted, runs into tens of thousands every year and is part of the national culture.

You want to be famous for five minutes? All you have to do is go out and shoot someone – or, better still, two or three people on successive days – and watch the hysteria spread like wildfire on CNN, Fox News, NBC, CBS, ABC and the local stations, turning an event of tragic but limited significance into an all-consuming national and international emergency. Your success will be measured by the number of satellite trucks that you can attract to the scene of your crimes. The written press, more television-aware than it used to be, will take up the hue and cry. In next to no time even a serious newspaper such as the *Washington Post* will be offering its readers a catalogue of tips for staying safe: 'While outside, try to keep moving . . . Walk briskly and in a zigzag pattern . . . If you are fired on in an open area, drop to the ground and roll away from where you were standing.'[6]

This is not a plea for censorship but for a sense of proportion. The sky will not fall in on us. World peace is not threatened by a gunman's rampage in Montgomery County, Maryland. Yet, as the networks tell it, it might as well be. They never learned the art of understatement. Hype and hysteria are their preferred modes of expression. Terrorism and television feed the frenzy of each other's appetites.

This is even more true of the new terrorism than the old. The TV networks, and especially the rolling news channels, are its means of communication. The broadcasters and the terrorists have much in common besides their mutual dependency. They have countries of origin but are not state-sponsored and their functions are essentially stateless. They communicate both internally and externally through the latest technologies, in which they are highly literate. Their messages cross borders.

Just as much as the BBC or CNN or al-Jazeera, al-Qaeda also describes itself as a network and is programmed to reach an international audience. Television is its transmission vehicle – what the politicians call 'free media' – not paid for except through acts of extreme and sacrificial violence. Without the platform that the broadcasters provide it would be little more than a faction of bombers. With this platform, the faction of bombers becomes a player on the world stage of greater importance than most sovereign states. Those who plan and coordinate their attacks have the additional satisfaction of sitting back and watching their handiwork unfold on television. Alone among the global audience, they know when to switch it on for the big bang. Since they planned the spectacles that rolling news cannot ignore, they are in a real sense its schedulers. The networks provide them not only with a showcase, but also with a sense of validation: the event was real, *because* it was all over CNN – and continued to be, for months and even years. This was Rimzi Binalshibh's account, broadcast on al-Jazeera a year after the event, of watching American Airlines Flight 11 crash into the North Tower: 'An operation like this you see in front of your eyes in that manner! The brothers thought that this was the only operation. We said to them: "Be patient, be patient," and all of a sudden there was Brother Marwan ripping through the South Tower of the World Trade Center in an unbelievable manner.'[7]

The masterminds of terror have the further satisfaction of observing from afar their effect on the networks themselves, which amplify the hysteria of a nation under siege. They clear the decks of all other news. They stamp their output with full-screen slogans such as 'WAR ON TERROR' or 'AMERICA FIGHTS BACK'. They fly the flag, mix journalism with patriotism (always a dangerous combination) and instil a sense of panic among the people. Terror provokes counter-terror, which in the case of the Administration's response to 11 September – wars in Afghanistan and Iraq, in short order – had the full and unquestioning support of the news media. The side effects included unbalanced reporting, the curtailment of civil liberties and the stigmatization of ethnic groups, such as Afghans and Arab Americans. This also played into the terrorists' hands. A 'round-up-the-usual-suspects' mind-set takes over in these circumstances: the Oklahoma City bombing of 1995, initially speculated to be the work of Muslim fanatics, was actually carried out by Timothy McVeigh, a home-grown extremist of the so-called 'patriot movement'.

Journalism needs to think long and hard about how it deals with these challenges. The campaign against terrorism will not end this year, or next year, or any time in the foreseeable future. I expect it to be with us, in one form or another, for generations to come. It is past time that the TV networks considered their role in it – not as cheerleaders for tougher counter-measures, but as trustworthy channels of information in difficult times. The rolling news services have special responsibilities. They are defined by F-words. They aim to be first and fastest with the news. Their nature, too often, is to be fearful, feverish, frenzied, frantic, frail, false and fallible. Some mistakes are bound to be made, as they always have been, by journalists seeking to discover the truth in the fog of breaking news; but those mistakes do not have to be as *systemic* as they have become in the rolling news business, when rumour masquerades as fact, and networks compete wildly with each other to get their speculation in first.

Again, this is not a plea for censorship, but for a measure of self-criticism and a long overdue code of practice: that, especially in the coverage of terrorism, the broadcasters report only what they know and not what they guess; that they deliver bad news with less gusto and relish; and that they subject their governments' responses to impartial and critical scrutiny. That is what journalism used to do before terrorism unhinged it. There is much to be said for a return to its first principles, in which the test of excellence is not 'We got it first!' but 'We got it right!'

5

'Take Me With You, Please'

A New Beginning

For every door that closes, another opens. The door that closed for me was the one to the House of Commons – the same door that Black Rod smites so mightily at the opening of Parliament. Having kept a promise to serve the people of Tatton for only one term, I took the Independent cause instead to Brentwood and Ongar in rather unusual circumstances and ran a strong second. (To be more specific about the circumstances would be to invite litigation: it is my misfortune that, whenever I stand for Parliament, I tend to attract the attention of litigious people.) We were always going to run out of money or time, and in the end we ran out of time: given another week, we might just have done it. We had a great campaign going and a terrific team of young people with us – more volunteers than all the three main parties put together. There is no automatic support for an Independent. Every single vote must be wooed and won, and we garnered more than 13,500 of them. I am actually prouder of what we did in Brentwood against all the parties than in Tatton against the rather dodgy candidate of one of them. Neil Hamilton was any candidate's ideal opponent. I couldn't call him corrupt then, but I can now, since he was found to be so twice in a court of law. I hope that I was gracious in defeat – or at least more gracious than Neil Hamilton had been four years earlier. The most memorable concession speech in electoral history was delivered by an MP, confident of his popularity, who had never for a moment expected that the voters would desert him. 'The people have spoken,' he said, 'the bastards!'

My own reaction was different. It was one of sadness for my supporters but relief for myself. I left the count in the soft light of dawn, held a press conference and drove to Suffolk to accept the presidency of the Japanese Labour Camp Survivors' Association. I told those old soldiers, who had suffered such a terrible ordeal and were now mostly in their eighties, how honoured I was to be in their company; and that, perhaps for the first time in my life, I understood the meaning of liberation.

The door that opened was UNICEF's. I had already been enlisted in their parliamentary supporters' club, and had undertaken a couple of expeditions for them as an MP, one to Kosovo and the other to Burundi. My companions in Burundi, the harder of the two assignments, were Hylton Dawson and Oona King, two of the small band of Labour MPs whom I really admired. I even broke non-party ranks and endorsed Hylton Dawson in his re-election campaign in Lancaster, which he won against the odds; but I am baffled and saddened to this day by Oona's support for the Prime Minister's war in Iraq. It was unfathomably out of character. Politics is unnerving like that. It can take people you know, or think you know, and persuade them to do the strangest, daftest things. Politicians walk on trapdoors; but they don't have to make it as hard for themselves as they do.

In July 2001 UNICEF asked me to become one of their goodwill ambassadors – unpaid, of course, and part-time. They had a rather grand title for it: Special Representative for Humanitarian Emergencies. The reality was more prosaic. They needed someone who could look after himself in the unquiet corners of the world where they wouldn't wish to risk the lives of their A-list celebrities, film stars and the like, whose presence there might have seemed even more superfluous than mine. Most of the good things in my life have happened by accident rather than by design, and this was certainly one of them. I had never planned a career path that might include becoming the poor man's Robbie Williams or Roger Moore; but if that was what UNICEF wanted, I would willingly agree to it. Sir Alex Ferguson, the Manchester United manager, signed on with them a year later, on a unique free transfer, and for the same reason. Their cause is impossible to say no to.

It was also a privilege to keep the company of Bill Deedes. At the time I joined, this peer of the realm, former Conservative MP and editor of the *Daily Telegraph*, was already eighty-eight and one of UNICEF's most active special representatives. Probably the most distinguished journalist of our time and others before it, he expressed a quaint and touching anxiety about what the *Telegraph*'s proprietor, Conrad Black, might think of his weekly column. Conrad Black, also a peer of sorts, should surely have been more concerned about what his senior columnist thought of *him*. A few months earlier, at the scene of an earthquake in Gujarat, Bill Deedes had suffered a mild stroke. His friends put it down to an unbalanced diet, too much coffee and not enough Scotch, out of deference to Islamic sensibilities. He recovered and returned to the fray on assignment for UNICEF and the *Telegraph*, but better provided with life's elixirs. This he did successfully in Pakistan a year later. Because of his age and courtly demeanour, and the deference with which he was treated by the UNICEF staff, he caused a great stir in a refugee camp where Afghans mistook him for their exiled king, who was actually a year younger. I was a generation behind, and happy to act as Bill's supporting cast.

In a reasonable or peaceful world UNICEF wouldn't exist. It was set up after the Second World War to alleviate the plight of children, so many of them orphans, in and around the battlefields of Europe. The United Nations Children's Fund is not only still in business but now more urgently needed than ever in an overcrowded, disaster-prone and turbulent world, marked by all kinds of conflicts, except the war to end all wars, which is still awaited. The soldiers can look after themselves but the children cannot. Because the immunity of civilians is a thing of the past, the groups of people most at risk in armed conflict are the very old and the very young – the old because they are unable to escape the onslaught, and the young for precisely the opposite reason: the energy and curiosity that direct them towards it. This is what makes children the most vulnerable to anti-personnel mines and cluster bombs. The unexploded cluster bomb especially, painted and glittering, invites them like a toy just waiting to be played with. Except that it isn't a toy. Whoever finds it becomes its victim; and, like its cousin the landmine, it knows no ceasefire. The new world disorder has its own curriculum. It says a lot about the times we live in that across the world, from Cambodia to Angola, the very first lesson a child needs to learn – because without it there is no point in learning any others – is mine awareness and identification.

Another sinister novelty, and the issue in one of UNICEF's long-running campaigns, is the phenomenon of the child soldier. The sacrifice of childhood has become a feature of the wars of collapsed states, especially in Africa. Sierra Leone and Liberia have provided the most terrible examples of young victims and orphans of war being thrust into uniforms and armed gangs, or exploited as saboteurs, couriers and spies – and the girls turned into sex slaves. In the Iran–Iraq war of the 1980s, six-year-olds were offered martyrdom as minesweepers. The use of child soldiers, not previously widespread since the Middle Ages, was made possible by developments in small arms technology. The old .303 Lee-Enfield, the British soldier's stand-by until 1958, was too heavy and cumbersome to be in any sense child's play. You could be run through with a bayonet while you tried to reload the five-round clip into its magazine. It was the infantry's enemy as well as its friend, and I was one of those cursing it. The drill sergeants loved it: all that you could do with it efficiently was slope and shoulder arms on the parade ground. The modern global equivalent, the Kalashnikov or AK-47, is lighter, simpler and easy enough for a boy of twelve, or even younger, to handle. Mikhail Kalashnikov himself, now living in retirement in Russia, is reputed to have said that he wished that, instead of the assault rifle, he had invented the lawnmower. Would that he had. But it would have made no difference. The need and the technology coincided; and the same weapon, or something like it, would have been made and traded under a different name. Mr Kalashnikov didn't benefit much financially at the time, because his invention was never patented, but at least he earned his place in the dictionary; and because his rifle was a byword for efficiency, he then signed up with a German company, which wished to put his name on a range of its knives, umbrellas and snowboards.

The Afghan Border

There was no lack of causes and campaigns for UNICEF's newest recruit; but where to start? The obvious place, in the autumn of 2001, was Afghanistan. Twenty years of war and three years of drought had produced a humanitarian crisis of the gravest proportions, even before the destruction of the World Trade Center in New York and the global crisis that followed. The catastrophe of 11 September provoked the instant threat of American reprisals against the Taleban regime, which harboured the world's most wanted man, Osama bin Laden. Hundreds of thousands of Afghans, starving and desperate, tried to flee the country across closed borders. The UN expected two and a half million in Pakistan alone.

UNICEF is not a faint-hearted outfit. My minders hit upon a scheme to send me out on the first flight with a cargo of aid from the warehouse in Copenhagen to Peshawar. Nearer the Afghan border, they promised, the supplies would be ferried across mountain passes by a convoy of 2,000 donkeys.

'Really 2,000?' I asked incredulously. The BBC had expected logistical miracles, including crossing closed frontiers and unbridged rivers, but had never offered me a single donkey, never mind 2,000, with which to perform them.

'Well, maybe 800 at the very least,' they answered, 'but not less than that. There's no other way of getting aid to that part of the country.'

My lack of riding skills has been with me since the age of eight, when I was thrown off my father's horse with my twin sister Sylvia (each of us remembers that she caught the other); but maybe a donkey would be easier. Journalists are by nature expeditionary people. I could never resist an adventure, and it sounded an inviting prospect, until security clearance was denied at the last moment. On the plane, off the plane – just as in the old days; but I took comfort: this time I was being messed about by people I really admired. I was out of war reporting for good, and not obliged to compete with forty other BBC correspondents in and around the Afghan borders. UNICEF offered an alternative and more rewarding way of going to the wars.

On 8 October 2001, the Americans (with token British support) struck back at Osama bin Laden and his hosts in Afghanistan. Bombs and missiles hit training camps, bases and airfields in Kabul, Kandahar and Jalalabad. After that the Americans were asked if they had run out of targets. '*We* didn't run out of targets,' they answered; '*Afghanistan* ran out of targets.' They were faced with the pointlessness of blasting a million-dollar missile at a five-dollar tent. It was the very opposite of a target-rich environment.

Taleban sympathisers rioted across the Pakistan border in Quetta. They attacked the UNICEF compound and set fire to offices and aid vehicles. *Classic Martin Bell timing*, I thought. *No sooner do I agree to join UNICEF than it finds itself in someone's line of fire.* My motto comes from the Book of Job 5: 7: 'Man is born unto trouble, as the sparks fly upward.'

UNICEF was not deterred. Within two weeks it found an equally challenging destination – a constellation of islands on a dry river bed along the desolate border between Afghanistan and Tajikistan. It was a no-man's-land twice over. Thousands of refugees had fled there from a part of northern Afghanistan under Taleban control a year earlier, and as the fighting had intensified, they had been joined by thousands more. The flood plain of the River Pyandzh, where they had sought refuge, was inhospitable to any form of life except the river grasses. It offered them nothing – no fuel, no food and no water (except from the river under Taleban fire). It offered no escape either. The Tajikistan border to the north of them was closed. Their plight was as desperate as any I had come across in all my war-zone wanderings.

Every war throws up its anomalies, and this was one of Afghanistan's. As if in a throwback to the Cold War, its border with Tajikistan was guarded and sealed not by Tajik but by Russian troops. In terms of realpolitik it was as if nothing had changed. It was frozen in time as the southern rampart of a country, the Soviet Union, which technically no longer existed. From their border posts on a high escarpment, the Russians with their tanks and artillery looked down on the human catas-trophe of the unprovided Afghans. The mismatch between power and need was tragic, and typical of turn-of-the-century politics; but the Russians had relented enough to allow two aid organizations in for limited periods and on specific missions. The two were UNICEF and the British medical charity Merlin, which was carrying out a programme of immunization among the refugee children.

We travelled down from Dushanbe, the capital, through the dustbowl of southern Tajikistan. It was a desert that had been irrigated by the Soviets but was now neglected and returning to its original condition. Where the watermelons sprang from was a mystery. They were offered to us as breakfast by our hosts from Merlin, just short of the border, where the dust blew in our faces under the trees between the end of the road and the broken troughs of the irrigation system. Drought knows no borders, and it didn't need a war to make an emergency. A million Tajiks were threatened with starvation that winter.

UNICEF's purpose was to help the afflicted, both directly and by raising awareness of the gravity of the crisis, both on the border and across it. Governments can and will do only so much, and even that in line with their political agendas. The rest depends on philanthropy and fund-raising, and without publicity fund-raising is all but impossible. So the party included a news agency TV cameraman, a photographer and Alice Thomson of the *Daily Telegraph*, who is one of those people – and they aren't so many – who persist against the odds in trying to give journalism a better name than it has. She is among her paper's rising stars and a regular adornment to its masthead. She is also younger and easier on the eye than the other columnists; but it was her reporting skills and her way with words that accounted for her rise through the ranks from secretary to associate editor.

None of this impressed the stone-faced Russians. Not only UNICEF, but even the CIA, with its strapped suitcases full of dollar bills, was having difficulty gaining access at the time. The KGB's long hand reached out to the border post, and the list of those authorized to pass it did not include the journalists. It was to Alice's credit that, in the report that she filed, she did not claim to be where she wasn't; yet her account of the Afghans on the islands was as vivid as if she had been down there among them.

Not being a journalist any more – an ever-growing advantage, I found – I was one of those whose names were on the list. We surrendered our passports to the Russians as a guarantee of good behaviour, and our convoy of Toyotas and Land Rovers ground down the escarpment to the plain below in choking clouds of dust. It was like a lunar landscape with river grasses – the first invisible refugee camp that I had ever seen (or rather, not seen). It had no tents or wire, or perimeter or security guards. It was not so much a camp as a sort of wildlife sanctuary, spread out over miles across the islands. Only if you looked closely did the place decode itself. Some of the grasses had form and shape – rushes woven together into the palisades of the compounds where 10,000 refugees eked out an existence and the women remained hidden.

The only substantial structure was a brick factory. Men were trying to build huts against the winter weather, but the homes for most people were holes in the ground with only the grass for protection. Merlin's secret weapon was Valerie Powell, from Cornwall, six feet tall and a living figurehead of authority and compassion – the sort of woman who once did heroic things on the borders of an empire, which was exactly what she was doing on the borders of this one. A trained midwife, she was all that the refugees had, under Russian sufferance, by way of a doctor. When they improvised a clinic for her, she was too tall to stand up in it until they raised the bamboo ceiling by a foot; but mostly she had to find the women, who were too reclusive to find her. 'It's like looking for birds' nests in the Norfolk Broads,' she said.

Where the refugees didn't establish a camp, the two aid agencies did. They laid out their chairs and trestle tables on the dry river bed, surrounded them with plastic fencing, and went to work immunizing 350 children against measles, polio and diphtheria. Some of the kids were suffering from scurvy and the effects of malnutrition. A few came running out of curiosity, the rest were brought in by their fathers and brothers; the mothers stayed out of sight. The winter cold was setting in. Each child was rewarded by UNICEF with a blanket, a winter jacket and a woolly hat. It was the only good thing that had happened to them for months. The war they had escaped remained uncomfortably close. The wind died down, and the still air was stirred by echoes of explosions from the other side of the river. From the force of a hard-dying habit, I supposed that they were rocket-propelled grenades.

There was, of course, a language barrier. It was bridged partly by the unspoken and universal language of compassion and partly by the aid agencies' gifted Tajik staff. A girl of about six, less shy than most, had learned from one of them the only phrase of English that she wanted. She looked up at me with her shining brown eyes, as if at someone from another world (I was not dressed like a Tajik and was the most obviously foreign person there), and repeated it: 'Take me with you, please,' she said. It caught on like a chorus among the others: *'Take me with you, please.'*

Now, how do you answer that? In the misery and desolation of the Pyandzh Valley, *how do you answer that?* I did not, because I could not. Although my friend and former rival Michael Nicholson of ITN had once done something of the sort in Sarajevo's orphanage, the Afghan border was a different matter. The UN's own rules on the transfer of refugees were strict, and even if they hadn't been, the Russian border guards would certainly have prevented the spiriting away of any of the river people. We emerged disconsolately to brief Alice Thomson and the others, and to try to get them access the next day. That was also met with a Russian veto.

Bearing Witness

The Hotel Tajikistan in Dushanbe, to which we returned, was the war reporters' frantic rear headquarters. It was a scene hardly changed since the Ishmaelia (Addis Ababa) of Evelyn Waugh's *Scoop* more than sixty years earlier, all a bustle with combat-jacketed characters coming and going in a state of high anxiety, loading and unloading, cursing and cajoling, and conspiring with or against each other, as hacks do. The air war had already started and they were planning their personal ground campaigns. TV reporters, the most competitive of the species, eyed each other warily like beasts of the jungle. John Simpson, who had passed through just ahead of me, saw it in much the same way: 'Like rats in an inadequate cage, we bared our teeth at one another and tried to guard our small pile of wood shavings.'[1] Nearly all the exclusives in news are on foreign frontiers, and this was an opportunity for correspondents to outshine each other that would occur, on average, only once in a decade. There was a professional pecking order, and reputations would rise or fall according to how they fared. Earlier in the crisis, a charter plane full of the big names of television trying to get to New York had been unkindly dubbed 'Ego One'. With the exception of Bosnia, where we had uniquely tried to help each other, war zones seldom bring out the decency, if it ever exists, in the journalists assigned to them.

The hotel door swung open and the BBC's veteran cameraman Tony Fallshaw burst through it, trailing half a ton of techno-baggage as dusty as his beard. Even the most clean-cut of my former colleagues started to look like the Taleban after a while. Tony and I had worked together across Europe from Belfast to Bosnia. He had just spent a month in the dire conditions of a tiny enclave in Northern Alliance territory. It offered the prized dateline *'inside Afghanistan'*, but not much else by way of comfort or access, and was miles from the nearest front line. I must have looked about as welcome as Banquo's ghost.

'What on earth are you doing here?' he asked.

'UNICEF stuff,' I answered.

'But not news any more? Don't you miss it?' They always asked that, as if news were an addiction as hard to shake as nicotine or alcohol.

'Not at all,' I answered truthfully. It had lost its hold. I was free of it.

'Not even a little bit?'

'No, not even a little bit. I've done my time. It's over.' I had no more nostalgia for it than for the House of Commons. There are things in life that you do for one reason or another, like caring about them or earning a living, and then let go without regret. I think that it's called growing up.

The Hotel Tajikistan offered an amenity that had never been

available in the other war-zone watering holes, the Continental Palace in Saigon or the Camino Real in San Salvador (still less the Holiday Inn in Sarajevo, most addictive of them all, which seldom had electricity). In the lobby of the hotel stood a television screen tuned to BBC World, the BBC's equivalent of CNN, but with a more global and less national agenda. CNN, under threat from Rupert Murdoch's Fox News, a rightward-leaning competitor, had lost its edge and become an echo of the voice of the White House. The BBC was more independent, but its coverage of the Afghan crisis mainly consisted at that time of correspondents on hotel rooftops exchanging guesswork, by satellite and at great expense, with other correspondents on other hotel rooftops. The curse of rolling news had spread worldwide. Rooftop journalism doesn't even resemble the real thing. It operates on the wrong level. It isn't down on the ground, where real people live and real news happens. Thanks first to politics and then to UNICEF, I was lucky to make my escape as it took over.

The UNICEF function was actually much the same as the reporter's: bearing witness. There were only two differences. One was that, having shed the cloak of journalistic neutrality, I was no longer an objective observer but an unrepentant advocate – with nothing to apologize for in speaking for an organization that worked for all the world's children. The other difference was the transmission system. Instead of the satellite feeds to London for the BBC, I wrote and gave speeches and interviews (nineteen of them, one after the other, on my return from Dushanbe) for UNICEF to whoever would listen – a bit like the Ancient Mariner, I suppose, who 'stoppeth one of three'. It was a sort of missionary work – spreading an awareness of the world's realities to audiences who might or might not be willing to listen. The words of Eli Wiesel seemed more relevant than ever: 'It is not because I cannot explain that you won't understand; it is because you won't understand that I cannot explain.'

I am sure that in the heat of the moment I exceeded the UNICEF remit from time to time. I described the crisis following the fall of the Twin Towers as a wake-up call for us all ... the most consequential conflict of modern times ... a time to make the case against indifference, the vain assertion of rights and privileges, the cold and timid souls who know neither victory nor defeat. I suggested that the new world order was more dangerous than the old ... that not even medium-term remedies were available to us ... that it was time to lift our eyes from the ground around our feet. I quoted liberally from Lincoln, Theodore Roosevelt and Churchill, and, from I know not whom, that we had the choice of living together like brothers or dying together like fools. Whichever organization invited me – whether the Churchill Club in Llandudno, the British Red Cross in Liverpool or the Ward of Cordwainer Club in the City of London – it did not escape the word from UNICEF, with war-zone variations.

If I had any doubts about these enterprises, they had to do with a sense of guilt, quite common I believe among professional aid workers (which I was not). Like lords of the universe, we would drive around on our field trips in four-wheel-drive juggernauts, growling air-conditioned Toyota Land Cruisers with vast antennae and top-of-the-range radio sets, communicating both with each other and with mission control in the capital. Our convoys, operating in the cause of all the world's children, would swirl dust into the eyes of eight-year-olds on the roadside staggering under their burdens of firewood – the very people we were supposed to be helping.

The doubts about the radio communications were stilled by what had happened in Burundi. Our host there on the parliamentary visit in 1998, the UNICEF Representative Luis Zuniga from Chile, was murdered by rebels in a refugee camp a short while after we left. UNICEF was not only an agent for good. It was also a target of violence, from Bujumbura to Quetta to Baghdad, and had a duty to do what it could to protect its people. Modern vehicles and radios were part of this protection. I accept that, but I'm still not sure about the added value of the air-conditioning. Security is one thing, and luxury another.

An unpaid job can be more rewarding than a paid one. The UNICEF term of service, now extended for a further two years, provided a privileged insight that I would never have had as a reporter – an insight into the politics of aid and development; into what happens to a country in crisis after the TV cameras have moved on; into the dedication of the agency's staff and the difference they can make to children's lives, whether because of the UN's prestige or in spite of its bureaucracy; and into the ever-growing chasm between the overdeveloped and underdeveloped worlds, a constant source of tension and reproach. The people being helped by UNICEF, and those from whom it sought its funds, seemed to belong to different planets. One week you would be among the destitute on the Tajikistan–Afghanistan border, where an onion was a luxury and eye-drops were being used as cooking oil. The next, thanks to Uzbekistan Airlines' magic carpet, you would be spirited to London to keep the company of the fashionable and bejewelled, wined and dined at a benefactor's mansion, entertained by world-renowned musicians doing their bit for UNICEF – and all credit to them for doing it. My role was that of an intermediary, master of ceremonies and teller of uncomfortable truths, the witness from the war zones, trying to translate one world to the other and make sense of it. I found it harder than anything in television, which is a medium with an unseen audience. Above the melodies for cello and violin, 'The Swan' by Saint-Saëns and a 'Chaconne' by Bach, I heard the voice of the brown-eyed girl on the border, quietly at first, but then in crescendo: *'Take me with you, please'*.

6

Malawi

New Variant Famine

Imagine a country in which more than half the eleven million inhabitants are children. Imagine a country in which half a million have died of AIDS and where there are half a million AIDS orphans. Imagine a country where the number of cabinet ministers (forty) is greater than the average life expectancy of the people (thirty-nine). Imagine a country where so many are dying, and dying in their prime, that a quarter of its education budget is spent on teachers' funerals. Unfortunately, you do not have to imagine such a country. It already exists – or at least it did in 2002. And then the crops failed.

The crop failure was the worst since 1949 and caused by the further plagues of flood and drought. Torrential rains had washed away the seasonal plantings of maize, the nation's staple diet. The second planting had withered in the fields. In a perennially poor country – one of the ten poorest in the world, and without even the alibi of armed conflict – millions would be left without enough to eat until the next harvest, if there was one. Malawi was on the edge of a great famine – and a new kind of famine, because the able-bodied young adults, the providers for their families, were especially at risk from the scourge of AIDS. AIDS and famine, sometimes described as the ugly sisters of Africa, connect with each other in peculiarly lethal ways. Dr Alex de Waal, Director of the UN's Commission on HIV/AIDS, identified the result of their interaction as 'new variant famine': 'As younger women – traditionally the main caregivers in society – die, the burden of care increases beyond the coping capacity of communities and families to the point that communities and families as a whole begin to sink into states of collective pathology.'[1]

In the countries worst affected – Malawi, Lesotho, Swaziland, Zimbabwe, Mozambique and Zambia – the 'ugly sisters' claim one life every minute.[2]

Famine was not a word that governments and relief agencies usually liked to use. They preferred the timid euphemism 'food insecurity'. I had no hesitation in using the F-word about Malawi, on the grounds that it was both truthful and expressive. George Orwell, the champion of plain English and enemy of doublespeak, would surely have approved. I remember having called a famine what it was in a report from the Indian state of Maharashtra during a severe drought in 1973. A state official reproached me.

'It isn't a famine,' he said.

'Why isn't it a famine?'

'Because we only had famines when we were ruled by the British. These days, it's a scarcity.'

The mission to Malawi, of which I was nominally the head, was actually led by David Bull, the astute executive director of UNICEF in London. It included Sarah Epstein, a patient UNICEF press officer, Mark Jordan, a rising star of Five News (and as multi-skilled as I was not – he was a reporter on assignment as a cameraman), and Neil Darbyshire, the executive editor of the *Daily Telegraph*. Neil was an old hand and former crime reporter who had risen in the ranks, like a sergeant major taking a late commission as an officer, to be number three in the *Telegraph*'s gentlemanly hierarchy. He was in the mould of my grandfather, Robert Bell of the *Observer* in the 1930s, a nuts-and-bolts journalist who put out the paper while the editor, J. L. Garvin, was busy grazing at grand political dinner parties. I am sure that today's *Telegraph* is edited otherwise, but Neil is clearly one of its safest pairs of hands.

UNICEF field trips come in three different categories, only one of which causes difficulty. Visits to the agency's projects by donors and MPs are relatively easy to organize, even to areas of recent conflict. I had been on a couple during my political episode, to Burundi and Kosovo, and could then speak more effectively for UNICEF, both in the House of Commons and out of it, from personal experience. It is the third category, involving the press, that tends to be troublesome. Journalists are troublesome people. It is what they are paid for: to break down the doors behind which the truth lies hidden, and not to take no for an answer. It is not enough for them to tour an agency's clinics, feeding centres and water projects. They want to see for themselves what the problems are – unannounced, off the beaten track and at the sharp end. They will demand to know who is to blame for the state of things. Frictions will arise when the host government is in a state of ignorance, or even denial, about the problems on its territory.

The government of Malawi was in a state of semi-denial. Only under international pressure did it declare a state of emergency. It then admitted that there was a food shortage, but assured the people they would all be fed, even while some of them were already dying. A compliant press echoed the official assurances. Malawi was by no means the worst-governed country in Africa. It was ruled in security terms with a relatively light touch and could even boast a measure of democracy; but the United Kingdom, by far the greatest donor of aid, had cut off more than £12 million in budget support because it had been spent on unaccounted items such as ministerial limousines and foreign travel by officials of the ruling party. The Danes, whose ambassador had been expelled for outspokenness (and for other reasons peculiar to Danish politics), retaliated by closing their embassy and cutting off all aid, including half the salary of the national football coach. Worse than that: eighteen months before the crop failure, the government had sold off its food reserve of 167,000 tons of maize, stored in former tobacco warehouses in Blantyre. Its defence had been that the grain was deteriorating, and it was under IMF pressure to reduce its debt; but the outcome was that when the food reserves were needed, they didn't exist. There was no maize to put on the market to drive down the price. And there was a further mystery about the proceeds of the sale. An investigation by the Anti-Corruption Bureau revealed that most of them had gone to senior politicians, who had sold off the grain and pocketed the profits in their new capacity as maize merchants. One of those accused of enriching himself was the minister responsible for poverty alleviation. The United Nations, which isn't famous for plain speaking, openly criticized the mismanagement of the grain reserve.

You couldn't help wondering – at least I couldn't, without my UNICEF hat on – what hope there was for a country where nine-tenths of the people lived in poverty, yet where the airport at the largest city, Blantyre, boasted a VIP lounge for government ministers, a VVIP lounge for visiting heads of state and a VVVIP lounge for the President himself. From this arose Bell's Law of the Delusions of Grandeur: a country's degree of mis-government is in direct proportion to the size and splendour of its airport VIP lounge. The United Kingdom's, to its credit, is a nondescript shed with a flagpole at Heathrow.

Malthusian Tendencies

Africa's disasters are characteristically produced by the waywardness of nature compounded by the wilfulness of man. In Malawi, the sale of the grain was man's contribution, as were the lack of irrigation and the failure to diversify into other crops besides maize. A portion of the blame may be traced back to the time before independence, when Malawi was Nyasaland, a sleepy British colony; but as for today ... 300,000 tons of grain would be needed at least by the autumn and 485,000 tons by the winter; a truck could carry 28 tons at most; only an unprecedented logistical operation, by road from South Africa and by a re-engineered railway from Tanzania, could save millions of Malawians from death by starvation, *if the world had the will to save them*. I was no longer sure that it had. The amount of aid pledged so far was only a fraction of what was needed. So many famines ... so many conflicts ... so many images of the mute beseeching eyes of starving children ... so many emergency appeals – a condition of donor-fatigue set in, especially in relation to Africa, and, in the stupefied world of the new journalism, the TV cameras, the engines of the aid effort in previous campaigns, tended to stay away on the grounds that African disasters were now so commonplace as to be no longer news. The cameras would be back, of course, when the famine had reached the equivalent of an 8 on the aid agencies' Richter scale, but by then it would be too late. The absurdity of it was that people had to die before they could be saved.

In my experience of Africa, which started with the overthrow of Kwame Nkrumah in Ghana in 1966, I had gone through the whole continental gamut from hope to despair. The hope had survived even the wars in Nigeria and Angola, and the antics of Idi Amin, one of whose weddings I attended on bended knee (it was to Lady Sarah, of the Mechanized Suicide Regiment of the Ugandan Army). The despair arrived with the AIDS epidemic and the ruination of Zimbabwe, and stayed. Maybe Malthus was right. That grim English economist, in his *Essay on the Principle of Population*, had set out to prove that the increase of population would only be checked by famine, war and disease – and indeed, that those plagues were necessary for that purpose. At the dawn of the new century there was something Malthusian about the plight of Malawi, which had been spared no scourge but armed conflict.

As an old Africa hand, I checked myself for this tendency to despair. Despair is not an appropriate state of mind in a UNICEF special representative. Nor is it prudent to criticize a host government with which a UNICEF field office does business – an office which, almost invariably, occupies the headquarters of a failed government enterprise. I took my cue from David Bull, who dealt with these things adroitly – especially over the disastrous sale of the food reserve.

'Who's responsible?' he was asked, after a visit to a feeding station in Blantyre, where mothers of undernourished children were receiving scoops of a life-saving blend of ground maize and soya beans. His answer was both diplomatic and truthful: 'The causes of this crisis are complex,' he said, 'but whoever is to blame for it, it certainly isn't these children.'

At Kasungu, in the famine's heartland, we paid a courtesy call on the Administrative Secretary. It was a very short call. She had other things than famine on her mind that day. She was the temporary custodian of two chairs with red-leather coverings, which stood at the side of her office. They were very grand chairs – indeed, they were more like thrones. They had been transported that morning from the capital, and the President and First Lady would occupy them in the afternoon at a rally of the ruling party, the UDF. The party's colours were yellow, and its women supporters in their yellow dresses were parading past the coffin shop on their way to the rally. The making of coffins was not only the country's most thriving business; it was its only thriving business.

People were dying on the way to the hospital, some of them carrying their infants for up to seventy miles. A hundred women with their babies crowded into a ward with just eight beds. A child was in traction, injured on the journey when his exhausted mother had fallen on him.

I asked, 'Are there children dying out there from lack of food?'

'Yes, there are a lot of children dying.' said the nurse.

'Every day?'

'Every hour.'

A Malawian social worker told us of a couple who had sold their baby for just under £3 in order to have one less mouth to feed, and to be able to buy food for their remaining children;

and a village chief, just back from a funeral, made a plea to the world through his visitors from UNICEF.

'We have only one thing to ask,' he said. 'It is that you save us, because we are dying.'

I saw the presidential rally the next day on Malawian television. It was a speech choreographed with much chanting and stick-waving; but for all its relevance to the here and now, it might as well have been held on another planet. It certainly had nothing to do with the reality before us, which was the fate of a dying people in a dying country. At home we would probably call it spin-doctoring. Malawi isn't the only country whose leaders place a premium on presentation, and pretend that things are not as bad as we think they are. The art of political smoke and mirrors is not confined to Africa. Spin-doctors, like witch-doctors, make a living by making magic and exploiting those who wish to believe in it.

At the insistence of the journalists Neil Darbyshire and Mark Jordan, we scrapped a planned day of rest and tourism and set off at random to the centre of the country, where the drought was most acute. Nothing stirred. The dry, unharvested stalks of maize stood like the wisps of effigies in silent fields. I had seen such things before, of course, for where there are crops there will be crop failures from time to time, even in prosperous countries like the United States; but nothing so extraterrestrial and lifeless as this. It was the first time in my travels that I realized that death has a sound, which is the sound of absolute silence.

In the first village we visited, a community of thirty souls, two had died of illness brought on by malnutrition; and in the next village, another two – and this in a country where, officially, there was food for everyone and no famine was acknowledged to exist. A smallholder took us to the graves, and spoke of the difficulty of finding survivors with the strength to dig them. The symptoms of starvation were bloating, chest pains, weakness – and then death. He had lost two relatives, one to AIDS and the other to famine, and now was the head of a family of sixteen children. They were living on banana roots, pumpkin leaves and the husks of maize that would in normal time have been fed to chickens, if they had any. The total absence of livestock deepened the silence. Malawians describe their fields as gardens. There was only one crop that the barren garden still yielded: field mice. On the way from the graveyard the farmer found a hole and started digging for them; scrabbling around in the roots of the maize stalks, he and his family came up with twenty mice of all sizes, which would either be eaten or sold. They were easy to catch: even the mice were weakened by the famine. The farmer thought that our presence had somehow brought good luck. We recompensed him for his time, but not for his mice, for which he could find a market. The going price for mice, which are a delicacy in Malawi, was fourteen to the pound!

At the roadside we met a woman who was on her way to a funeral. I asked Godfrey, our UNICEF guide, if we could attend it. He was doubtful.

'There could be a problem of protocol,' he said.

'There can't be a problem of protocol in just asking,' I replied.

There wasn't; but to my embarrassment the village chief insisted on bringing me a chair to sit on, almost as grand as the President's, from which to watch the funeral. Chairs matter in Malawi. The chief wanted the UNICEF representative to see what his people were living and dying through. There had been thirty deaths in his small group of villages since the crops failed. His people were a long way from the capital or any other centre of population. They had seen no aid and been offered none. It was, nonetheless, an occasion of great dignity. The men stood on one side of the clearing and the women on the other. Malawians keep their families segregated and their children away from funerals. The man they were burying had died of an illness made incurable by malnutrition. There would have been hymns and a service if he had been religious, which he was not. But he was respected as a good man, a main man in the village, well known for helping others. Amid the ululating grief of relatives, a village elder in a dark suit spoke the eulogy. He was a man in his forties: 'I had hoped he would be burying me,' said the elder; 'instead I am burying him.' They took a collection for his family, a pile of small coins from the poor to the poorest. I added a banknote to them, feeling like a waste of space and knowing that in the absence of a miracle – I couldn't work one, but could UNICEF? – the funerals would multiply into daily events as the famine took hold.

The food crisis was not as severe in all parts of the country – it would have been possible to visit the less affected areas and hardly be aware of it; but for Malawians whose crops had failed, it was just like being in a hospital and waiting to die. A victory for Malthus perhaps – born in 1776, died in 1834, and finally vindicated in a small and plague-ridden African country in 2002. There may have been grounds for hope out there somewhere, but I was damned if I could see what they were.

States of Failure

What am I doing here? Of what possible use can I be? In the face of an epic scale of misery on each of my UNICEF expeditions, both as MP and roving ambassador, I had been assailed by such feelings of guilt and self-doubt, but those feelings were especially acute this time. Through it all, I was certain of one thing: that if the necessary aid were not forthcoming, future historians would mark out the early twenty-first century, and this region of southern Africa, as the time and the place where the rich and powerful of the world finally gave up on the poor and wretched. If that were to happen, we would earn our right to a place in whatever hall of shame awaits the indifferent; and we would not only be failing those we should help: we would also be failing ourselves. Had not we, the British, been the most international people since the Romans? And would we now, in the face of these calamities, become the most withdrawn and insular?

On the way back I quizzed a friend about the politics of the place. He was a man of high intelligence and ideals, who had been a university teacher before becoming an aid worker. He was just the sort of person his country needed in government; but it is an unwritten law of politics that many of those who should go into it don't. (The reverse of that is also true – and not only in Malawi.)

'Was there ever a golden age in Malawi?' I asked him.

'Perhaps there was,' he said, 'and if there was, it was in the five years after independence – a new country then, no longer a colony or part of an unworkable Central African Federation. It had Dr Hastings Banda at the helm, who was an elder of the Church of Scotland, and the people really believed in him. There was no AIDS in those days, either, and a smaller population to be fed.'

As we cruised past the stricken crops for mile upon mile, my companion embarked on a passionate history lesson about the betrayal of hope, the failure of democracy and the political trajectory of the increasingly autocratic Dr Banda, who became president for life until he was overtaken by senility. Of the founding fathers of African independence, only Felix Hou-phouët-Boigny of the Ivory Coast outlasted him; and the Ivory Coast was no shining example, either.

'Then there was democracy,' said my friend, 'and a fresh start under a new leader in 1994. It was also the end of the apartheid regime in South Africa, with which Dr Banda had cooperated (he did it openly and in the daylight, he said, while others worked with South Africa secretly by night). Again it was a time of great hope. We had vowed to have no more presidents for life, but a leader who would serve for two terms at the most and return to his place among the people, and be accountable to them.'

Once more the hopes were dashed. In thirty-eight years

Malawi had been ruled by only two presidents. (I had no criticism of that. In fifty years I have been reigned over by only one Queen.) President Bakili Muluzi, Banda's challenger and successor, could not be blamed for the drought and only partly for the famine; but he had presided over the grain sale and the extravagances of executive power, and his friends in Parliament – even in the so-called opposition – were seeking to amend the constitution so that he could serve for a third term. They had been rebuffed at the first attempt, but would try again. What goes around comes around. Another president for life was in the making. 'And the worst thing of all,' said this true voice of Malawi, 'is that millions of people have lost what is most precious to them: their dignity as human beings. You have seen for yourselves that in the struggle to survive they are competing with animals for animal food, the husks and the roots. The bonds of family life, so strong in Malawi, are being broken by all these calamities together.'

On returning to London, I filed two reports for Channel Five News, with which they led their broadcasts. For the love of UNICEF, which had countless lives to save in Malawi, I left the political dimension unexplored. That was because of a conflict of interest between the roles I was playing as reporter and as representative. Sometimes in life you make compromises, which I have never liked but which were easy enough to justify in the cause of UNICEF. How good the reports were I was not in a position to judge – TV journalists, like politicians, are famously incapable of assessing their own performances, but tend to hype them beyond their actual merit. The word was out, however. Someone out there was watching the Malawi coverage – not only mine but the BBC's and ITN's. Pledges of help poured into UNICEF. A month later, the Disasters Emergency Committee, a consortium of thirteen British aid agencies from Oxfam to Merlin to Save the Children, launched its Southern Africa appeal. The immediate target was $40 million. The time was desperately short. Eighteen years earlier Michael Buerk had moved the world with a single report from the famine in Ethiopia. Since then the media's attention had wandered aimlessly downmarket. It was the high season of *Big Brother*, which was playing to record audiences on Channel Four and was about to be followed – heaven help us – by *I'm a Celebrity, Get me out of Here!* on ITV. The world in the new millennium was harder to move.

Home and Away

I came home. It was harvest time. On a country road in Kent I drove for hundreds of yards along a road that was covered with the spillage of the harvesting. There was enough grain lying there to feed a Malawian village for weeks on end. I appeared on a series of drive-time phone-ins, on radio stations across the country, to answer questions about the famine and its effect on the people of southern Africa. 'Don't we have enough problems of our own,' asked some of the callers, 'to concern ourselves with the plight of people on the far side of the world?' The answer is that we don't. Compared to the problems that they have, we have none at all. We may come to look back on the time we live in as a sort of golden age (although I don't see it that way myself) and wish that we had been aware of it when we were blessed with it. Until then it is wasted on us. Or maybe war and terrorism will write its epitaph.

I returned to Malawi two months later. The famine was even more acute. In a village near Kasungu, an African missionary, Father Emmanuel of the Society of St Paul in Nigeria, told me that he had encountered the identical problem of persuading people at home to understand the realities in southern Africa. On leave in eastern Nigeria, where he had grown up in the Biafran war, he had preached in his former diocese to congregations who never ceased to complain about the daily misery of their lives. Nigeria has the potential to be the richest country in Africa. 'You don't live in misery,' he told them; 'you live in luxury. If you want to see misery, come with me to Malawi, and I will show you misery.'

Breaking a long-standing convention of laying every particle of blame on the former colonial powers, Father Emmanuel held some in reserve for his fellow Africans: 'The problem is that we have too many leaders concerned not to help others but only themselves. Even in Africa people are hoarding things. In the midst of this crisis *they are hoarding things* – so the majority are suffering while a few are enjoying.'

At some point in the shuttling between London and Lilongwe, I gave a radio interview that was heard by Caroline Fry, the editor of the magazine of the Royal Geographical Society. She commissioned a gifted photographer, John Nicholson, to document the effects of the famine in southern Africa. It fell to me in my UNICEF capacity to write the words to accompany his pictures. I met John in Malawi when he was finishing his assignment there and on his way to Angola. Something about frying pans and fires came to mind.

'It's all your fault, Martin Bell,' he chided, 'that I'm here at all.'

But he understood that this wasn't one of the cases – there had been some in Africa in the past – of aid agencies talking up the gravity of a crisis for fund-raising purposes. The present emergency was so severe that it was hardly capable of being exaggerated. John had just returned to the lodging house from the hospital in Lilongwe, and was pale and trembling with the shock of seeing so many children close to death.

Before leaving home, he said, he had talked about their plight to his six-year-old daughter, Maisie, and explained why she wouldn't see him for a month. She had a tooth loose, as six-year-olds tend to. 'Daddy,' she said, 'I want you to give my tooth fairy money to those children.' And so he did – 200 kwacha (about £4) to the mother of a malnourished child.

A small gesture perhaps – but small is not the same as meaningless. Not to be outdone by a six-year-old, I made a small gesture of my own when I came across the Chisomo Club (*chisomo* means grace), founded by Blantyre's charismatic Running Water Church and funded by UNICEF. It rescued the city's street children, some as young as four years old, from a life of beggary, petty crime and worse. In every year that passed, the numbers of street children doubled. The club gave them a roof over their heads, a sense of self-worth and even a football team. All that they lacked was a strip. I solved that problem by talking to my friends at Carrow Road. On my return visit I was able to present the children with a full set of Norwich City shirts, provided free of charge by a great-hearted football club. They were thrilled to be wearing the most distinctive colours in the English Football League. It was a total coincidence that they were also the colours of Malawi's ruling party.

It is one thing to bring a smile to the face of a child, another to tackle the causes and effects of Africa's gravest crisis. There are no figures on the numbers who died in the famine of 2002. That is the way with the famines and food insecurities of the twenty-first century. Many of the deaths went unrecorded. A village chief told me, 'We used to report all deaths to the police; but there were so many, that there seemed no point to it and we had no one to send to them anyway.' The UN's agencies, especially the World Food Programme and UNICEF, worked miracles in preventing the famine's death toll from rising any higher. By December they were keeping two million four hundred thousand Malawians alive – nearly a quarter of the country's population. The parts played by the British High Commission and the Department for International Development were also heroic. The provisional answer to my Malawian question, 'Is this where the rich and powerful of the world finally gave up on the poor and wretched?' was a hesitant 'No, not completely – or not quite yet.'

But the famine next time ... that's another matter. I am sure that neither the British Prime Minister nor the American President gave it a moment's thought when they let loose the dogs of war in Iraq, but effects of the enterprise spread as far afield as the destitute states of southern Africa. This happened in two ways, one of which was simply visibility. The plight of the six most afflicted countries disappeared for months from the world's radar screens. Carol Bellamy, UNICEF's Executive Director, timed a high-profile visit to Africa during the war to focus attention on a great humanitarian crisis that was 'reshaping the lives of millions of children and women, far beyond the lenses of most cameras'. 'Reshaping' was another United Nations euphemism. 'Devastating' would have been nearer the mark.

A still more serious consequence was the threat to the integrity of the United Nations itself. The war in Iraq was launched in defiance of the Security Council consensus and the UN Charter. The decision to use force prevailed over widely accepted concepts of international law. Those members of the US Administration and its advisers who were the most enthusiastic about going to war – Donald Rumsfeld and Paul Wolfowitz, among others – were also the most sceptical about a post-war political role for the United Nations, either in Iraq or anywhere else. Shorn of its political authority, the UN's purpose would then become strictly humanitarian. It would function as a sort of gigantic, glorified, globalized Oxfam. This would be devastating for its agencies across the world, and nowhere more so than in southern Africa. The World Food Programme, the World Health Organization and UNICEF work as effectively as they do because of their status as agencies of the United Nations. All the countries of the world, with one exception, see the United Nations as having an indispensable place in their future, and themselves as having an indispensable place in the UN's future. The problem is that the single exception is the world's only superpower. Take away those laws and rules and commitments, enshrined in networks of treaties and conventions, and whole continents will descend into chaos and anarchy, with Africa first to fall.

7

Yesterday's Wars

Back to the Future

Channel Five News is the newest, smallest, brashest and most innovative of the British television news services. Its reputation is for presentation rather than content, and it has inspired a slew of the most dreadful imitations. Founded in 1997 as an offshoot of ITN, it made its mark by breaking with the suits-behind-a-desk and cardigans-on-a-couch traditions of delivering the news. Instead it had its presenter Kirsty Young, who could woo a camera with eye contact like no one else in the business, perched on a ledge like the ones in bus shelters, narrow and angled so that people can't go to sleep on them.

Not that sleep was ever going to be an option in the frenzy of Five News. It was noisy and interactive, conducting its dialogue with the nation on the principle that the little guy shouts loudest. The agenda was remorselessly tabloid: health scares, celebrity divorces, royal mishaps, footballers' hairstyles, movie premieres, show business and orphaned animals. It prospered modestly for its first five years, rising to an audience of close to a million, and then surprised everyone by swerving, out-of-character, towards the higher ground.

Partly this was because the parent channel, in a shift of strategy, was attracting advertisers by shedding its image as the nation's soft pornographer; but it was also because so many of its rivals had followed it on the low road that it saw an opening on the territory they had so obligingly vacated. The style remained tabloid, but sometimes with the edge of a serious agenda. This may or may not have had anything to do with my reports for the network from Malawi, but it occurred to someone there that the reporters of yesteryear – some of us, I fear, believed to have departed from more than just the TV screen – might still have something to offer. Channel Five's Head of News, Chris Shaw, attacked the BBC's ageism, its obsession with youth and good looks: 'This represents a slightly thought-less conversion to a populist ideal, prizing presentational skills, fluency, grooming and good looks over conviction journalism.'[1]

'Every bulletin has young, good-looking people standing in front of walls of videoscreens. It's all a bit synthetic.'[2]

He then hired a handful of yesterday's news people, for what I thought of at the time as timewarp television by the dear departed, but what he more kindly described as 'classic report-ing'. Five of us were lured out of retirement with a combined age of 315. The text for the publicity photographs of the gang of five was: 'The good news is they're back – the bad news is they're only back for a week.' The age gap was alarming. Most of us had embarked on our TV careers not only before Channel Five had been launched, but before its regular staff had even been born.

Carol Barnes, formerly of ITN, used her experience as a magistrate for a well-informed report on law and order. Michael Brunson, who had been ITN's political editor, called for a complete restructuring of the House of Commons, to curb its chronic adversarial tendencies. Angela Rippon attacked the nonsense of conceptual art, in which I don't doubt that she spoke for the great majority of the British people. Sandy Gall and I were reassigned to former war zones. There was a symmetry to that: neither of us fell into the male model category and we were lucky never to have had to pass a screen test or stand in front of a videowall.

Of all my former rivals at ITN Sandy Gall was the one I most admired. He was a craggy veteran of foreign wars, who would sometimes dress as an Afghan in Afghanistan, but always as a man: he didn't do burkas. Sandy radiated dignity and integrity.

I regarded him as the gentleman in the whorehouse – by which I didn't mean to disparage my friends in the profession (the profession of journalism, that is), but only to suggest that some of the ITN reporters I had worked against were rather sharp characters whom I didn't find totally trustworthy. The height of praise at ITN was to be known as a good operator. 'Journalists,' said my grandmother, 'are a shady lot and seldom the sons of gentlemen'; and she should have known, because she married one. There was nothing the least bit shady about Sandy Gall. Now a courtly seventy-three-year-old, lame in one leg but with his curiosity undiminished, he was back on his old Afghan stamping ground to interview President Karzai and report on moves to rebuild the Bamiyan Buddhas destroyed by the Taleban. It was a tour de force that only he could have done quite as he did it, in the measured language and cadence of a natural broadcaster. His style and elegance had fallen out of fashion. The *Daily Mail* wrote: 'A blessed absence of frenzied arm-waving and exaggerated hand gestures made the return to the screen last night of famed TV reporter Sandy Gall a welcome relief from the agitated, neurotic style of some of his successors.'[3]

Of course, reporters with more past than future aren't always the easiest to deal with. Chris Shaw recalled, as a young producer on the frantic twenty-four-hour news cycle, asking Sandy for an update during the 1991 Gulf War. 'Sorry, old boy,' came the answer; 'don't do updates.'

It also made sense to revisit the scenes of past conflicts. Except in times of global commotion, television news has retreated from its foreign fields and provides a window on a much smaller world than it used to. Within its shrunken horizons it has the appetite, at most, for just one foreign crisis at a time. It is all or nothing for the news people. Either everyone is there or no one is. This baffles the viewers. Audience research has discovered that one of the things they most want to know is, after the guns fell silent and the press caravan moved on, what happened next? They are seldom told. It is as if these places somehow fell off the map. Just as yesterday's reporters can become non-persons, so yesterday's datelines can become non-places.

The closest thing to mission impossible in television is to infiltrate a post-war report, especially one about peace and reconstruction, into a regular daily news programme. By definition it lacks the magic ingredient known in the business as 'bang bang' – the combat footage which editors find irresistible. I confess to having used the sounds and images of gunfire myself, not because they had a great deal to do with the story I wished to tell, but because I needed them as an attention-getting device to have the damn thing shown at all. *No bang bang, no airtime* was one of the iron rules of war reporting.

The Fog of Peace

Forty years after starting in television, I embarked on an assignment that was more like a pilgrimage than a job of work. Since the Dayton Agreement, Bosnia had spent seven years in a state of ceasefire – peace was still too strong and settled a term for it. There was definitely no bang bang when I arrived in Sarajevo with Simon Fordham and Nick Porter of Channel Five, touching down on the runway where I had come under fire in June 1992 and been saved by good luck and the BBC's Vauxhall Carlton, which stopped a bullet as effectively as if it had been armour-plated. I wrote to Vauxhall and thanked them for making an armoured vehicle without knowing it.

There was no gunfire this time – and no roadblocks either, in a country where it had once been every man's ambition to own his own. Petrol stations were the thing to have now – great gaudy, glitzy gasoline geysers with supermarkets and brothels bolted on to the side of them, where the warlords and black marketeers had planted and tended their profits. When the shooting ended, they could still find other ways to make a killing. If wars were not so lucrative for the few who benefit from them, they would be harder to start and easier to stop.

The sprawling boom-town prosperity of Vitez, where British troops had been based ten years earlier and some had died trying to keep the peace, was especially shocking to someone who believes that in almost all circumstances peace is preferable to war. Vitez seemed to contradict that. It flashed out an electric message that said, *Never mind the bloodshed, give war a chance and you too can turn a quiet farming neighbourhood into a garish American shopping mall with Disneyland accessories and neon lights for all*. All that it lacked was the Stars and Stripes, casinos and slot-machines. Come back next year and it will probably have those too. But for the lives that were saved, if we had known during the war where Bosnia was headed, we might have walked away.

My first call was on Paddy Ashdown, who after a career in opposition now had more power than he had ever imagined or wished to use. He had picked up a couple of extra titles along the way. Lord Ashdown of Norton sub Hamdon, in Somerset, was also the European Union's High Representative, which sounded like something straight out of Gilbert and Sullivan. The job was a cross between colonial governor and constitutional evangelist, trying to cajole the distrustful leaders of three peoples and two mini-states to work together for the good of all. At the end of the war the Serbs had been bombed into accepting their own peace plan. The Dayton Agreement, granting them their self-administered territory inside Bosnia, was a recipe for deadlock, and none of the previous High Representatives had been able to break it. They had, besides, been men of uneven quality. One was described by an American general, to his face, as 'a third-rate diplomat from a fourth-rate country'.

The former Liberal Democrat leader, when he took the job in May 2002, inherited a considerable shambles. He loved it – even the shambles – because he loved Bosnia. He was planning to buy a home there. His idea of relaxation – only moderately popular with his bodyguards – was to go yomping across its mountains at weekends, starting out on an unmarked muddy

track that was the inter-entity border. We strolled to his office –
in so far as one can stroll with an ex-Marine who believes that
a flight of steps is an assault course – through streets that had
been the most dangerous in Europe and the open market that
had been the scene of two of the war's notorious massacres, in
February 1994 and August 1995. He reminded me that, during
one of his wartime visits, I had told him that leaving Bosnia
gave me a feeling like being kicked in the stomach. For both of
us, I believe, it was the one country besides our own that we
loved the most. Was I getting too close to it, perhaps? In my
kind of journalism, so long as you are fair, you are allowed to
do that. Nor is it unprofessional for a war reporter to harbour
a passion for peace. I had always wanted to work myself out of
a job. Paddy felt the same way about his. He was aiming for a
Bosnia that would no longer need a High Representative.

After six months in office, his honeymoon was over. The
Russians objected that he was pushing too hard, and they still
had an advisory role through a diplomatic relic of the war called
the Contact Group. The Serbs complained that he was pro-
Muslim, the Muslims that he was pro-Serb and the Croats that
he was definitely anti-Croat. We passed a news-stand with a
satirical magazine on it showing him in a cartoon embrace with
Radovan Karadzic, the Bosnian Serb leader wanted for war
crimes but still at large. He shrugged it off as the sort of libel
that went with the territory. 'The two biggest problems I have,'
he said, 'are the impatience of the international community and
the refusal of so many people here to see how far they've come.'
He listed the achievements: the freedom of movement, the return
of refugees, the reconstruction that was finally making Sarajevo
look like a peacetime city. (He might have added the traffic
jams: peace and freedom can be defined as the peace that makes
traffic jams possible and the freedom to be stuck in them.) But
the Dayton Agreement was fundamentally unworkable. There
was little economic activity except for organized crime, foreign
aid and government jobs, some of them superfluous. There

was no tourism either, although an ex-war zone is actually an excellent place for it, offering a warm welcome, attractive prices and a fascinating recent history with new ruins alongside the old. Bosnians had fallen into gloom and doom, their favourite modes of being. An optimistic Bosnian is the rarest bird in the aviary.

Was there also perhaps a lingering element of nostalgia for the siege? It sounds a strange idea but not out of the question. It can happen with wars – that those who fight in them and survive them develop so strong a sense of comradeship and common purpose that the years of armed conflict, however terrible, become ingrained in their consciousness as the best of their lives. They will never share such extremes of feeling again. It was the same with the veterans of the Normandy landings: they were soldiers then, and for some of them everything after-wards became an anticlimax. There are people for whom the simplicities of war – us against them, good against evil – are preferable to the complexities of peace. War is for heroes and peace is for politicians. There is also the question of self-image; as Dr Johnson observed, 'Every man thinks meanly of himself for not having been a soldier.' Almost without exception ex-soldiers are proud of having served; even I am, and I didn't do much but shoulder arms and move pins on a map. Recon-struction was further inhibited because many young, well-quali-fied Bosnians, who had fled abroad in the early days rather than stay and fight for one side or another, found it difficult to return and face the question: 'What did you do in the war?'

In his office above the former front line, Paddy Ashdown put forward a theory that was neither liberal nor democratic, but actually more of a colonial governor's theory, rooted in what happens in the aftermath of conflict: there can be such a thing as too much democracy. When wars end, in Bosnia, Kosovo or just about anywhere else you can think of, the West believes that what these countries need first and foremost is immediate and abundant elections: just wave the magic wand of democracy, set the people free to elect their own, and all will be well. 'Look at what we did here,' he said: 'we held elections all over the place and as soon as we could, for assemblies and councils at all levels of government. What we should have done was put law and order first. Once that is in place, you have the foundation for a real democracy.' The same mistake was made in Iraq in 2003. Liberation without law and order is not much of an achievement. It merely replaces tyranny with anarchy.

The lawlessness began at the highest levels. The international regime in Bosnia was undermined by its failure to arrest the two most prominent Bosnian Serbs indicted for war crimes at The Hague. Ratko Mladic and Radovan Karadzic were still at large, Mladic probably in Serbia and Karadzic flitting across the border between Bosnia and Montenegro. He had eluded two attempts to lift him, probably as a result of tip-offs from within the ranks of the NATO force that was supposed to do the lifting. His defiance of the law enhanced his stature and encouraged Serb hard-liners in their mini-state. He was an unlikely hero – a man who loved Sarajevo so much that he bombed it. It took a great deal to turn this incoherent poet, undistinguished psychiatrist and mediocre politician into a mythic figure; but the Stabilization Force had somehow managed it. The American Jacques Klein, one of Paddy Ashdown's partners in the power structure, properly called it a scandal.

I had come across the fog of war before, but never the fog of peace. That was how murky the future appeared from the vantage point of the Jewish cemetery, which of all the war's battlefields had been the scene of the fiercest fighting over most of the three and a half years. It was new ground for me. I had never been able to get near it before, but had watched from afar as the parachute flares illuminated it and the tracer fire blazed into it and across it: Sarajevo's fireworks shows were like none other on earth. Now the mines had been removed and the synagogue was under repair, but most of the tombs were still shattered. It was one of those rainbow days which distil Sarajevo's essence and make it one of the most special places on earth – squalls and sunshine, snow on the mountains, crowds in the coffee shops, muezzins and church bells calling the faithful competitively to prayer, dancing waves on the Miljacka river, dark scudding clouds pierced by shafts of light illuminating the acres of graves and new minarets, the changed face of the city. Sarajevo tears at the heart-strings like no other city on earth. Its defining music is Albinoni's 'Adagio', played by its mournful concert hall cellist Vedran Smajlovic. I never knew a place with so many moods and so many cemeteries. Bosnia could easily go either way, to peace or war, or remain on the perilous middle ground between them. When Paddy Ashdown arrived, he had told the Bosnians that a fork in the road lay ahead of them. Now he warned them, 'We have come to that fork in the road. You have the choice of living in a modern European state or a Balkan backwater. No one else can make that choice for you. You have to make it. And the time to make it is now.'

The European option was by no means a lost cause. Journalists are fond of gloomy predictions along the lines of 'You think this is bad? You ain't seen nothing yet – it's about to get worse.' This kind of world-weariness is thought quite falsely to indicate experience and the golden quality of gravitas to which all hacks aspire, especially in television, where appearance and reality are more or less the same. It is endemic not only to war reporting but even to weather reporting: how seldom does a piece about flooding not end with the forecast of more floods on the way? I have played the pessimist myself, and in one respect already the Bosnians proved me wonderfully wrong. I always thought it unlikely, after the upheavals of 1992 and 1993, that a significant proportion of the hundreds of thousands of refugees driven from their homes would ever return. So many of their own people had been killed by neighbours, in the most cold-blooded and appalling circumstances, sometimes even a bridegroom by his best man, how could they ever trust those neighbours again? This applied not only to the Muslims in the north and east of the country, but to Croats in the centre and to Serbs in isolated communities everywhere. No side had a monopoly of injury and suffering. A more likely outcome was the permanent separation of Bosnia's three peoples: a Balkan apartheid.

The return of refugees was slow to start, especially in the Drina Valley where many of the worst atrocities occurred, but in some areas it turned from a trickle to a flood. Prijedor was one of them – and an unlikely place, too, since it once had the reputation of being the capital of ethnic cleansing by the Serbs. During the war, they had rounded up all the Muslims and Croats they could find – sizeable minorities in Tito's Yugoslavia of brotherhood and unity – stripped them of any possessions of value, carted them off in trucks and buses and dumped them on the nearest front line, which was near Travnik fifty miles away. The refugees were obliged to pay 400 German marks each as a sort of departure tax, which was actually a survival tax – the price of not being killed. Thousands of others, mostly men of military age, were not so fortunate: most of the bodies have still not been identified, and many have not been found. The north of Bosnia was mining country, and mineshafts were a favoured disposal site. The homes and places of worship of all these people, the living and the dead, were blown up after them. It was the Serbs' way of claiming the territory as their own, and denying – even to themselves – that they had ever shared it with anyone. They had done the same thing in Croatia, obliterating ancient Catholic churches at Petrinja and Erdut. They had a gift for redefining their history and geography, and making things happen in ways that would come back to haunt them.

The UNICEF Corrective

This Balkan-style final solution, however, wasn't final at all. I had the extraordinary experience, ten years later, of revisiting the Prijedor municipality and finding that 17,000 of its Muslims and Croats had returned – and not only that, but that the younger Serbs and local officials were reaching out to welcome them. *Things don't always go from bad to worse.* Minarets were back on the skyline. Entire communities were being rebuilt, often with German government money, since many of the refugees had fled to Germany, and both they and their hosts had an interest in their return. They were, of course, nervous and frightened. 'Months later,' said an aid worker, 'they still have a refugee mentality, they tend to keep themselves to themselves and who can blame them, but we are learning to live together again more than I would have ever thought possible.' The aid worker, the UNICEF coordinator, was herself a victim of the war. She was a Serb from Croatia, who had lost her husband, also a Serb, when he had been murdered by a drunken Serb soldier nowhere near a front line.

War is such a multitude of private tragedies that you sometimes need an anti-depressant to cope with them. Mine is called UNICEF. It is where good people make good things happen in almost every corner of the world. So I briefly slipped into my role as goodwill ambassador to visit the Lighthouse Club in Prijedor. Accommodated in a municipal building provided by the Serbs, and funded by UNICEF, it was a place where the young people of all communities could work and relax together. The activities included computer training, drama, painting, music and even break-dancing – the club had come third in the national break-dancing championships. A twenty-year-old Serb was teaching computer animation to Muslims and Croats – his friends, as he described them; 'It doesn't matter where they come from, we are all friends here, from all groups of people, and why should we not be?' The club members were young people whose childhood had been confiscated, but were old enough to have been aware of what was going on around them. War for most kids is something they see only in the movies. No such luck for these: it was something they survived first and made a movie about afterwards. The film was an animated computer-generated cartoon of their personal experiences – the burning houses, the tanks in the streets, the tyranny of the Kalashnikov, the ordinary young men of the village turned into killers. There was an especially effective sequence that showed the soldier boys becoming robots, before recovering their humanity. The children of conflict perceive it in very special and vivid ways: their image of war is a house on fire, and their image of peace is a house with flowers outside it.

The message of the movie was one of hope: these young people had come through such a nightmare that they would work together to prevent it ever recurring. That was the good news. The bad news was that most of them believed that, because of the lack of a functioning economy, they were being educated for a future that wouldn't be there for them in any foreseeable Bosnia. According to an opinion poll, 67 per cent of the young were convinced that they would have to go abroad to make a living.

This connected with Paddy Ashdown's attempt to kick-start the economy into something like life. He set up what he called the bulldozer committee, to clear away the bureaucratic controls inherited from Titoist Yugoslavia. To open a restaurant, for instance, it was necessary to obtain sixty-eight permissions, including one from the Ministry of Defence. More serious was the corruption. People who might have been interested in start-ing up businesses were deterred by the need for other and whispered permissions from the dark side, the payoffs to extor-tioners and racketeers. That was a legacy of the war, not of the Communists. Paddy Ashdown saw it as a general post-conflict phenomenon, not peculiar to Bosnia, but much the same there as it had been in the ruins of Europe in 1945: 'Corruption stalks after war like a bright shadow.'

That is the point of paying attention to yesterday's wars. They may no longer be news but are not yet history. They won't stop affecting us when a ceasefire is signed, and the peacekeeping troops have gone home. Their impact will last for years and spread across borders. Either we help to stabilize those countries, especially the ones geographically close to us, or they will surely destabilize ours. They are already doing so. The handguns flooding Britain's inner cities come in many cases from Balkan bazaars, including Sarajevo's (the MACIO machine pistol is a favourite). So do people with the ability and willingness to use them. So do the drugs, the smuggled guns and (in some cases) illegal immigrants that connect with them. Bosnia is a trading post and depot for all three – the Wild West of the Balkans. Apart from a small amount of timber it has no other exports; but the exports that it does have spread trouble like the plague. The bog-standard British politician, concerned only with domestic issues and the early-day motions and press releases relating to them, should need no great visionary qualities to see that what happens in Bosnia today will affect Birmingham and Bristol tomorrow, and maybe his or her prospects of re-election.

Ghosts of the Past

Another way of learning from the past, for those who pay attention to principles as well as interests, would be to revive the Bosnian tourist industry by offering day trips to the storage facility of the International Commission for Missing Persons in Tuzla. As dry as old bones? You wouldn't think so if you went there.

It looked like a nondescript commercial warehouse, of the sort where Asda or Tesco might store their groceries, with a central corridor leading to offices on one side and what appeared to be the door of a refrigerator on the other. It *was* the door of a refrigerator. The temperature inside was kept constant at between ten and twelve degrees centigrade. The door creaked as it opened, like that of a castle in Transylvania, as if to give a warning that the secrets inside were unspeakable, which they were. Whoever entered would come out changed for life. Inside, on metal frames from floor to ceiling, stood orderly rows of white canvas body bags, neatly numbered, holding the remains of 4,500 of the victims of the Srebrenica massacre in 1995, and now awaiting identification and burial. A further 2,000 were stored in a salt mine, and others elsewhere. On a table in one of the offices was a collection of what were called 'commingled remains'. The earth-movers had been busy, and many of the bodies had been buried and reburied in attempts to destroy the evidence. Another office contained plastic bags with the personal effects – combs, banknotes, photographs, spectacles and letters – that the victims had had on them when they died. These were the equivalent of the glasses and shoes piled high in the museum at Auschwitz – a reminder that these murders were the greatest war crime committed in Europe since those.

My guide was an old friend, Gordon Bacon, who had run a small but effective charity, Feed the Children (now Children's Aid Direct), in central Bosnia at the height of the war. He brought a Geordie tenacity to the job: in an earlier life he had been an inspector in the Durham police. He was now Chief of Staff of the International Commission on Missing Persons, which had the task of finding and identifying the unknown victims of this conflict and others: it was also active in Serbia, Croatia, Kosovo and Macedonia. It had made little progress for the first six years, until advances in DNA science made accurate tracing possible. Between twenty and thirty of Srebrenica's victims were being identified every month. The names of more than 2,000 are now known.

'It matters,' he explained gently, 'because it ends the families' uncertainty about what happened to their loved ones. It gives them the grace of finality. It allows for burial if we can ever get a burial site; and because it shows that there can be no secret war crimes or unknown victims, it acts as a deterrent to the would-be war criminals of the future.' The failure to agree a burial site was another of the High Representative's inherited headaches. The mothers of Srebrenica wanted their husbands and sons to be laid to rest in nearby Potocari, where they had been rounded up outside the UN base and marched off to their deaths. The Serbs were resisting, on the grounds that it was their territory and a provocative place in which to establish a graveyard. The burials began in early 2003. The dispute was typical of a country where it sometimes seemed that the dead mattered more than the living – except that, in this case, the dead prevailed. When the Serbs relinquished their suburbs in Sarajevo under the Dayton Agreement, they became their own tomb-raiders and took out some of their dead with them. A brave soldier and good friend of mine, Major Milos Stankovic of the Parachute Regiment, coined a term for it: he called it 'necrowar'. It aptly described a conflict in which, even aside from the victims of Srebrenica, there were more than 20,000 other names on Gordon Bacon's list of the dead and the missing. And that was just in Bosnia.

It makes no more sense to brand the Serbs as an evil people for what happened in Srebrenica than to brand the Germans as an evil people for what happened in Auschwitz and Birkenau. The Serbs were also victims of massacres, in Bratunac, Kupres and elsewhere. War crimes are individual. The guilt is shared – unevenly, but still shared – between those who committed them and those who permitted them; and that surely includes the Western democracies who offered protection to the innocent without providing it. *Good things happen because people make them happen and bad things happen because people let them happen.* The lesson is the same: *nie wieder* – never again. Of course there is, in some, an instinct to murder; but is there not, in all of us, as powerful an instinct to save our skins when we can? As well as wondering what kind of people *they* are, should we not also be wondering what kind of people *we* are – who could have saved so many lives, but didn't?

8

Party Politics

Machine Politics

When the war in Iraq seemed inevitable, I ran into one of my friends from my time as an MP, a front-bench Tory of the courteous and old-fashioned sort who might have difficulty, these days, in finding a seat in Parliament. That was not a criticism of him but of his party. It was supporting the war as fervently as the government, if not even more so, partly because of the Tories' links with the neoconservatives in the White House and Pentagon. My friend looked deeply troubled. He disagreed with his party's policy, and described the build-up to war as the worst time in all his years in the House.

'What we are doing may not be wrong,' he said, 'but we are doing it at the wrong time and in the wrong way.'

'Then why don't you get up in the House and say so?'

'I'd like to,' he said, 'but I owe so much to my party, I just can't bring myself to do it.'

What kept him on board was not so much his seniority – there is not much reward, financial or political, in a parking place on the opposition front bench – as his sense of loyalty to the party, in which he believed and to which he owed his safe seat in Parliament. They had found it for him and they kept him in it. He will be an MP for life unless the party implodes. The Conservatives, apart from their leadership struggles and a chronic tendency to form themselves into circular firing squads, are especially strong on party loyalty. Until 1997, it was a strength that made them the natural party of government.

The war in Iraq was not only a failure of diplomacy. Most wars are failures of diplomacy. It was also a failure of politics, and especially the politics of Britain's two main parties. This was brought home to me most vividly a few weeks before the conflict when I chaired a debate in front of a thousand sixth-form politics students in the Central Hall, Westminster. The Conservatives were represented by Michael Ancram, their foreign affairs spokesman, and Labour by Adam Ingram, the Armed Forces Minister. These were respected and professional politicians making their parties' cases for war in the gloom of the great auditorium; but as the students saw it, they were out there on their own in a debater's no-man's-land. From the questions the young people asked and the way they reacted, when they applauded and when they sat on their hands, I had the impression that not a single one of them supported the forthcoming war. If I had been Michael Ancram or Adam Ingram I would have asked myself, 'Where did we go wrong here? How have we failed to make the case? What does it say of my party's *connectedness* if it cannot take the young people with it on such a vital issue of war and peace?' Today's sixth formers are tomorrow's voters. They were not apathetic, but passionately engaged with an issue that mattered more to them than even tuition fees. Chairing the debate, I had a sense of the country's future slipping away from the magnetic fields of the two main political parties.

I cannot remember an issue on which party politics seemed so remote and out of touch as it did on the Second Gulf War. The two House of Commons votes, supporting the war on a split decision, were hailed by the government as the democratic mandate for it. Yet they did not reflect the will of the people so much as the interests of the payroll vote and of MPs whose only careers were in politics. The party system creaked under the strain. The rebellion was led by the nationalists, the Liberal Democrats (strangely hesitant, as if they feared being accused of opportunism for doing what was right), a number of senior

Tories including Kenneth Clarke and Douglas Hogg, and more than the usual suspects of the Labour left – 139 Labour dissenters included many from the mainstream. A special mention in dispatches was earned by Graham Allen, MP for Nottingham North, who had been a Labour whip in the 1997 parliament with special responsibility (so it seemed to me, from my position below the Serjeant-at-Arms) for intimidating the Liberal Democrats; he would stand over them at Prime Minister's Question Time, uttering sotto voce imprecations out of the starboard side of his mouth. In 2003, having escaped from the whips' office, he was the most articulate leader of the campaign against the war, a standing reproach to the party system, and one of those MPs – there should be more of them – who only really find themselves when they cast ambition to the winds and break out of the prison bars of party discipline. Within his party, he was accused of endangering marginal seats. Outside it, he was honoured at an award ceremony as Parliamentary Backbencher of the Year, and was all the more effective as a poacher because he had once been a gamekeeper. Without sin there is no salvation.

Part of the problem is the professionalization of politics. A new political class has come into being, with little experience of life outside the feverish precincts of Westminster. These are young men and women who complete their education (usually still at public schools and Oxbridge) with high ambitions, a good degree and even better connections; but they don't yet *know* anything. It would be good for them to find employment for a while as street cleaners, plumbers, or even (in an extreme case) lawyers. Then they would have experience to bring to the practice of politics. Instead they obtain jobs in MPs' offices or party headquarters, progress into the ranks of special advisers, and hope to be selected for a winnable seat before they are thirty. Half the Conservatives' new intake in 1997 belonged to this category. They were not like the Conservative backbenchers of old – a broader-based coalition of knights of the shires, farmers, ex-soldiers, lawyers and businessmen – but a new breed of pin-striped machine politicians unrepresentative even of the mass of Tory voters. Their emergence as a group reflects a disconcerting sense of the otherness of politics.

This leads into the issue of quality. There is a wider gap between the best and the worst in politics than in any other profession. Doctors, lawyers, teachers, soldiers – even some journalists these days – have to pass certain tests and acquire certain skills before they begin to practise their trades. All that MPs have to do is not to be a lunatic or criminal (although some of them come alarmingly close), and then, every four or five years, to submit themselves to the voters for election. It sounds democratic enough – and but for the party system it would be. It is the party system that, valuing loyalty above all other qualities, stuffs the backbenches with stooges. The parties themselves pay the penalty for it when they are voted into power, and find their ranks rather thin in MPs with the calibre to be ministers.

Those ranks are also thin in women and minorities. I am hardly well placed to make this case, since my non-party in the House of Commons, for as long as it lasted, was 100 per cent white, middle-aged and male; but the statistics are those of an unrepresentative democracy. 1.8 per cent of MPs are from ethnic minorities, and 17.9 per cent are women. Only 1 per cent of the population belongs to a political party, only 32 per cent identify with a political party, and fewer than 60 per cent cast their votes in the General Election of 2001. *Big Brother* attracts more votes than the European elections. At constituency level most parties are cliques and cabals. It is not unknown for a constituency association to be run by just five members – and for three of those to be at daggers drawn with the other two. The parties are themselves unfashionable and sometimes ill-tempered factions. Their volunteers are an elderly, dwindling band. They attract fewer people from a narrower range than in the past. They behave like obsolete, dying institutions. Our democracy cries out for their renewal.

John Diefenbaker, the former Canadian Prime Minister, recalled that for his first six months as an MP in Ottawa he asked himself, 'How on earth did I get here?' Then, for the rest of his time, he asked himself, 'How on earth did all these other people get here?' I was no great parliamentarian myself, and was bamboozled by some of the procedures from start to finish, but at least I obtained my seat by accident rather than by fealty to a party. Even today, when we need to be represented by the best, too many MPs are slotted into safe seats on the grounds of no discernible merit except a record of honest toil for their parties. Knock on enough doors, hand out enough leaflets, cast enough votes with your party's group on the council, and in time you too can qualify for the best club in town and a comfortable job for life, with benefits including a generous pension, free parking at Westminster, a riverside terrace, first-class travel and trips to faraway places. If deselected or defeated, some of these people would be unemployable. This makes them all the more inclined to follow the whips' instructions. They vote as if their livelihoods depend on it, which in many cases they do. The payroll vote is a term normally used of MPs of ministerial rank, and even those below them on the career ladder who support the government with their votes to protect their jobs; but it actually applies to all MPs within the party system. Although their salaries and allowances are paid by the taxpayer, they owe their well-paid positions to their parties and for all practical purposes are on the party payroll. The result is that, while many MPs of all parties are men and women of real ability and distinction, there is a higher proportion of creeps among them – that is on the minimalist definition of creeps, as people whom it is genuinely hard to admire – than there is in the population at large. The parties have an arthritic grip on the windpipe of democracy. The Scottish Parliament, by contrast, has a voting system which gives a fighting chance to smaller parties and Independents with a cause. Scottish politics is healthier for it, and Edinburgh's Parliament is more representative of the people than Westminster's.

Flawed systems produce flawed outcomes. An interesting example is the Cheshire parliamentary delegation, whose personalities I know quite well, because I used to be one of them. They are the same individuals in this parliament as in the last, except that my place as MP for Tatton was taken by George Osborne, a high-flying young Tory who probably knew more about the House of Commons when he joined than I did when I left. The Cheshire MPs offer an extraordinary range of ability, from the supremely talented to the totally hopeless. I yield to no one in my admiration for (and love of) Gwyneth Dunwoody, the Member for Crewe and Nantwich, who sets a fine and effective example of what an independent-minded MP can achieve within a party; she is hardly the pin-up girl of the whips' office, but is widely respected elsewhere. At the other end of the scale, the delegation includes two members who are such totally obscure, dim-witted, unregarded, unmitigated, irredeemable bottom-of-the-barrel mediocrities that, but for the backing of their parties, they would stand no chance at election time of saving their deposits or after that of finding any sort of a job. Like the Admiral in *HMS Pinafore*, they always vote at their party's call and never think for themselves at all; they are little known in the House of Commons and even their own constituencies; but their votes count as much as anyone else's in making our laws, or voting for war or peace (on the last occasion – the war in Iraq – both of them trooped obediently into the war lobby). They are machine politicians – and the machine is so outdated, defective and inefficient that, if it were a car, it would long before now have been traded in for a new one. Or more probably junked, for lack of a trade-in value.

Like all old vehicles close to breakdown, political parties are expensive to maintain. They spend more money than they can safely raise. For the foreseeable future in general elections, the two main parties, Labour and Conservative (and for how much longer can the Conservatives escape relegation from the major league?), will try to amass a campaign war chest as close as possible to the new legal limit of about £17 million. (It depends on the number of seats they contest, and neither directly contests seats in Northern Ireland.) £17 million is less than they spent in 1997, but more than they can raise through retail politics from the rank and file of their membership. So they court big money. They practise the politics of reward and remuneration. They turn their conferences into trade fairs, where sponsorship is for sale to the highest bidder, and (for a fee) a lobbyist can lunch at a cabinet minister's table. They solicit contributions from wealthy individuals, many of whom, by an extraordinary coincidence, are honoured with knighthoods and peerages. Even the Liberal Democrats, who fund their campaigns more modestly, find tangible ways of thanking their benefactors. Indeed in a sense they started it. The systematic sale of honours in modern politics was inaugurated by Lloyd George. When I tactlessly pointed this out on the floor of the House, Charles Kennedy objected to the disobliging reference to his predecessor: he slipped me a little note that said, 'Your application for membership is cancelled!'

Parties are already funded by the taxpayer to an extent that most taxpayers don't know, and would be appalled by if they did. Opposition parties can finance their research out of 'Short money' (which has nothing to do with the size of the payout, but was named after Ted Short, the Labour Minister who introduced it). Further payments have been made through the Electoral Commission, both to mainstream parties and to smaller parties such as the Reverend Ian Paisley's Democratic Unionists. Only Independents are excluded from this largesse, which many politicians wish to see extended to a system of full state funding. The Tories, to their credit, disagree; but Labour has been sufficiently embarrassed by its cash-for-access scandals to see the attractions of a subsidy by the taxpayer.

This isn't an easy case to make. It would take a rare feat of oratory to convince the voters that money that could go to schools or hospitals should flow instead into the campaigns of political parties. Unwilling to make the case itself, the government found a surrogate advocate in the Institute for Public Policy Research, a think tank that acts as a pilot fish for the projects of New Labour. The IPPR's study obligingly concluded: 'There has never been a better time to introduce state funding for political parties ... The state funding of political parties alone will not usher in a renaissance of the mass political party and public confidence in democratic institutions. However, it can remove some sources of distrust in voters' minds and encourage parties to undertake more grass-roots activity.'[1] *Ho hum*, I thought, when the author of the study came to see me for the Independent perspective, which he duly sidelined when he came to write his report. The proposal penalizes small parties and Independents. Two questions are enough to demolish it. The first is: if the Lib Dems can run effective campaigns for less than £2 million, and the Nationalists for even less, why can't Labour and the Tories? The second is: if a party is in trouble, does it really make sense to expect its opponents as well as its supporters to bail it out? The argument falls to the ground on its own demerits.

Independent Politics

There has to be a better way of proceeding, and there is. Its trail was blazed by the smallest and most successful party in the General Election of 2001. The Kidderminster Hospital and Health Concern Party (henceforth referred to as the KHHC) was founded as a pressure group to oppose the rundown of the town's General Hospital, threatened with having its acute services transferred to the scandalously over-budget and not-so-nearby PFI hospital being built in Worcester. The people of Kidderminster were up in arms, and felt abandoned by their Labour MP, David Lock, who had taken a job as a junior minister in the Lord Chancellor's Office and somehow become persuaded of the merits of the PFI hospital. (He knew of my interest in Kidderminster, strongly objected to it and was the only MP on whom I ever put the phone down.) A retired physician, Dr Richard Taylor, came to see me at the House of Commons in 1999 to ask whether I thought there was any point in the KHHC fielding a candidate at the next election – not as a gesture, but with the real intention of winning. In urging them to do so, I quoted Vaclav Havel, President of the Czech Republic and one of the few political heroes of our time. 'Politics,' he said, 'can also be the art of the impossible.'[2] Richard himself became the KHHC's candidate in Wyre Forest, which is the Kidderminster district. I knew he could win, and joined the actor John Fortune in speaking for him at a packed election rally in the Town Hall. (As it turned out, I needed his help more in Brentwood and Ongar than he needed mine in Kidderminster.) What was astonishing was the scale of his victory, a majority of 17,000 over the established parties, the largest opposition majority in all England. It was a popular insurrection, a demonstration of the art of the impossible and the only romantic, heart-warming result in the most featureless General Election in living memory.

What was also astonishing was the economy of it. The budget for the KHHC campaign in Wyre Forest was a modest £4,872. Labour spent nearly twice that at £9,595, as did the Conservatives at £9,572. Break this down into costs per vote, and the figures were even more remarkable. Richard Taylor's votes cost 17.1 pence each as a cheese-paring democratic return on election expenses, Labour's cost 88.4 pence and the Conservative's £1.02. The Independent's politics, because they were cheaper, were well within the power of his supporters to finance. People gave to the party, as they would to a charity, not for personal gain or to further a business interest, but because they believed in the cause. This should be the model of future funding, not only for new and single-issue parties, but for the long-established and mainstream parties as well. Give the people something to believe in – an idea, an inspiration and a common cause – and they may well be persuaded that it is worth signing a cheque for. It mobilizes the idealism of ordinary people in a cause that brings them together. But offer them only politics as usual – machine politics, pork-barrel politics, I'm-in-this-for-what-I-can-get-out-of-it politics – and they will not be inclined to part with a farthing to fund it. The parties will then be forced either to run their campaigns more cheaply, which it is against their natures to do; or, more probably – because this *is* in their natures – to turn again to tainted sources and big-money contributors, either in the House of Lords or on the way to it, because they have no other means of financing their extravagant spending habits. People will then become even more alienated and less inclined to vote. We are now at the turning point. Either we succeed in renewing our democracy, or we watch it slide away from us down a slipway of sleaze and cynicism.

The problem isn't apathy. The Apathy Party wins elections, time after time, only because the alternatives are so spectacularly unattractive and ill-natured. Once, when I was on a radio programme with Richard Taylor MP, we were joined by a politician who had been soundly defeated in a seat that he should have won and that his party had held for generations. As soon as I was introduced, he denounced me as a miserable hypocrite. I never respond to insults, but I thought that this was a strange one. I could have been a happy hypocrite for all he knew. His response intrigued me. It was symptomatic of a tendency by otherwise reasonable people, when they become party activists, to press the abuse button at the drop of a slogan. They have only two gears: 'attack' and 'destroy'. Voters are alienated by this, as they are by the ritual hostilities of the House of Commons. The Society for Electoral Reform appointed a Commission on Candidate Selection, chaired by Peter Riddell, the Political Editor of *The Times*, to try to find ways of turning things round. It was clear to all of us (I was its token Independent) that the core of the problem lay with the parties themselves: 'The image of party politics is often unattractive. The traditional, and not always misleading picture, is of in-fighting among small groups, door-to-door canvassing on wet (never sunny) evenings, and interminable meetings about trivial issues ... The television image of politicians jeering or scoring points off each other ... does not encourage involvement and lowers trust.'[3]

There is nothing new in the mud-slinging. My predecessor as Independent MP, the great A. P. Herbert, was exasperated by it in what he called 'the rude Parliament' of 1945, the last one that he sat in: 'Whenever there was a big debate, there was such a *concerto* of nastiness and hate and imbecile yelling, that I thanked God, many times, that I was an Independent and could sit silently without disloyalty.'[4] The Parliament of fifty-two years later was no less cringe-making. Its characteristic modes of expression were the sneer and the snarl – the sneer from the government's benches and the snarl from the opposition's. I would sit there often on my little cramped cross-bench, some-times clutching a piece of quasi-medieval woodwork until my hand hurt to make sure I wasn't dreaming. I uttered quiet oaths to myself and wondered, what on earth was the point of this charade? What connection did it have with the real world? Why were these people behaving like this? How could it possibly advance the public good? It was, and still is, a defective model of politics, bringing out the worst in its partisans, and failing to deliver a Parliament that the people can be proud of. It was out of date even in 1945. In the twenty-first century it is the Jurassic Park of representative government. We have to move on to something less tribal and more constructive. The model is already available. The committee system of scrutiny shows what can be done when MPs work with rather than against each other, and form alliances across party lines.

Adversarial Politics

The adversarial model is deeply flawed. I had a dismaying experience of it, in law as well as politics, during my time as an MP. One of my constituents was Sally Clark, a Wilmslow solicitor who was convicted at Chester Crown Court, in November 1999, of the murders of her infants Christopher and Harry. It was one of the most notorious miscarriages of justice in recent times. I went to see Sally in her cell in Styal Prison just before Christmas 1999 – one of four Christmases she would spend in jail. I became convinced of her innocence, and supported her husband Stephen in his long campaign for her release. In 2002, microbiology reports were unearthed from Macclesfield Hospital – previously unseen by the defence and the jury – which showed that the second child Harry, like Christopher, had probably died of an infection. Yet right up to the Appeal Court hearing in January 2003, the prosecution failed to face up to the force of the evidence and continued to make the case for her guilt. For what possible reason, against all the principles of natural justice, could the Crown have wished to keep an innocent woman in jail? Was it a residual malevolence, a genuine belief in her guilt, or a last ditch stand to defend a reputation?

I think it was something more sinister and structural than that. Our courts, like our Houses of Parliament, operate on the adversarial principle. They are concerned more with arguments than with truths, which is why the silver-tongued advocates of the legal profession glide so easily and so often from one to the other. If you sit in the House of Commons and close your eyes as, in a state of disbelief, I sometimes did, you can tune in to the distinctive wavelengths of the 'honourable and learned Members', MPs who are also QCs. Bob Marshall-Andrews is exempted from this analysis; but for the rest, you can know them by their long-windedness, their facile and felicitous phrase-making, their insincere courtesies, their cut-glass self-confidence, and their ineffable ability to defend the indefensible, which counts as a priceless asset in party politics. They can as well succeed by defending falsehood as by exposing it. Indeed, in the courts they can succeed even better, advance professionally and win the admiration of their peers, if they can secure the conviction of the innocent and the acquittal of the guilty. This kind of lawyering, like this kind of politics, has nothing to do with right and wrong but only with making cases. In March 2003, Tony Blair made a brilliant case in the House of Commons for going to war in Iraq. As a parliamentary performance it was perhaps the best of his career; but it was based on false and misleading information. He too was once a lawyer.

The point-scoring ritual serves us as poorly in the Commons as in the courts. We accept it because the artful rhetoric and dispatch-box bravura, like Beefeaters and Horse Guards and Gilbert and Sullivan, are borne down to us on the great and flowing tide of our inheritance; they are like that for no other reason than that they always were like that. They are part of our sense of who we are and where we have come from; but they have outlived their usefulness and lead to unjust outcomes.

We are encouraged to think of party politics as an integral part of democracy. It is nothing of the sort. Candidates are commonly selected by a small clique of activists. In the European elections, they are listed in the order of the parties', not the voters', preference – a practice that might as well have come out of the rule book of the old Bulgarian Communist Party. The constituency link barely exists. Outside the ranks of party enthusiasts I meet no one who can identify a single MEP. Free spirits within a party are isolated and punished. Genuine Independents stand no chance – or so far they haven't; but the system has reached a point of such decrepitude that a non-party campaign might be a useful experiment in the art of the impossible.

As for the actual governance of the country, the outcomes are often arbitrary and distorted. Let us take the example – purely academic, of course – of a government with a large majority facing a weak opposition whose leader is believed, even within his party, to be an electoral liability. He is a figure of fun, and the party is doomed to defeat under his leadership. The government decides, for no very adequately explained reason, to embark on an unjustified, illegal and unpopular expeditionary war. It alienates many of its traditional supporters, who refuse to turn out for it at the local elections, and either abstain or vote Liberal Democrat. It damages public trust in public life. The opposition party thus achieves a considerable, if not overwhelming, victory at the polls; its leader, claiming credit for the success, cannot be unseated. It suits the governing party so admirably to keep him where he is until the next General Election that they might almost have contrived it, although no one would dare to suggest such brazen opportunism. In this way, through the mysterious workings of the system, a party can even turn its blunders to its advantage. The winners lose and the losers win. In such circumstances party politics does not express but frustrates the will of the people. No wonder they have wearied of it.

Outside the party system there is little evidence of apathy. On the contrary, citizen politics is alive and flourishing. People constantly involve themselves in causes and campaigns outside the rusted framework of party politics. In the run-up to an election, either local or national, new parties register with the Electoral Commission at the rate of twenty a month. They can be 'stop the war' parties, 'save our hospital' parties, environmental action groups or appealing oddities like the Idle Toad Party in the Ribble Valley. They may even be parties of the extreme left or right. So long as they remain within the law, these too have a right to campaign for a place in representative government. There is a word for it, and that word is 'democracy'.

A League of Decent People

The Independents cannot be a party – that would be a contradiction in terms, like a convocation of hermits; but they can be a political force for good, a fourth force in England and a fifth force in Scotland and Wales, which already have four mainstream parties vying for office. If there were not a niche for the non-partisan, there would not be two thousand Independent councillors in local government, elected without benefit of national advertising, taxpayers' subsidies or party political broadcasts. I have met them on the Independent Group of the Local Government Association. They are a league of decent people and the best of British. Of course, there are some odd characters among them, but no odder than those in regular party politics. The strength of the Independents is that they represent the people, not the parties. They practise a politics that is innocent of any ambition to enter the doors of Downing Street. They challenge the dictatorships of one-party states in such places as Middlesbrough and Mansfield, which they reclaim from the parties and for the people. They are close to their communities and judge every issue affecting those communities on its merits.

It is absurd that one party should claim a monopoly of wisdom for itself and a monopoly of folly for its opponents: life is more complex and interesting than that. It is equally absurd that, in local government, there should be a Conservative policy on street lighting, a Liberal Democrat policy on towpaths or a Labour policy on potholes (except perhaps to fill them in through a Private Finance Initiative task force). What Independents do from time to time to British politics is what Jesse 'The Body' Ventura, a former wrestler turned Governor of Minnesota, did to American politics: they blow a great blast of fresh air through it.

In February 2003, the senior elected Independent, Richard Taylor MP, held a non-party conference in his home town of Kidderminster. It was no trade fair. The lobbyists and tycoons were absent, but the league of decent people was present in force. They were Independent councillors and candidates for the Scottish Parliament and Welsh Assembly. One of those candidates, Dr Jean Turner, went on to win a famous victory in the Scottish Parliament. My difficult task, as the keynote speaker, was to raise their enthusiasm while urging them not to overreach themselves.

At the local level, Independents are a serious force. At the national level – including not only Westminster but Edinburgh and Cardiff – they are more of an Alka Seltzer. They purge the system when party politics fails, as it did in Tatton in 1997, in Kidderminster in 2001, and as it does in Scotland and Wales from time to time when the parties ignore the voters. If it fails again, we shall return to the fray. Our fires are banked but still they burn. We fill a gap in the democratic process. It is good for the political health of the nation that the machine politicians should feel threatened from time to time. We help to keep them within a certain range of honesty. When asked if I shall stand again, I used to take refuge in the Michael Heseltine formula: 'I can foresee no circumstances under which . . .'; but times change and party politics has fallen into such disrepute that, sometimes, I can glimpse the outlines of those elusive 'circumstances under which . . .'. One of the lessons that I learned from Tatton was never to say never.

It is necessary to hold the Independent corrective in reserve, as a warning to parties that, when sufficiently provoked, the people can rise up against them. I hope that future parliaments will have more than a lone Independent – with two, we could even form a group; but the party system is here to stay, and the future of all parties depends on reaching beyond their dwindling band of volunteers and attracting a new generation of voters, supporters and candidates. That means easing their disciplines and changing their cultures. It means making them less repugnant to free spirits. It means connecting with the idealism of the young. It means rethinking what they stand for, in terms of principles as well as interests. It means reviewing their ways of working: a young person from an ethnic minority, interested in making a political difference, is likely to be deterred by the language of politics in an old-style branch meeting – the points of order, composite resolutions and general procedural stuff and nonsense. As the Electoral Reform Society's Commission put it, 'If a broader range of high quality people from all sections of the community can be selected, and then elected, then public respect for our political system may recover and satisfaction with what Government does may also revive.'[5]

I entered Parliament without prejudice. I was a political innocent and had only set foot there once before. I had never thought about being an MP until twenty-four days before I became one. I had no preconceptions about political parties, either for them or against them. I left Parliament four years later with many new friends, and a few new enemies. What dismayed me most about the parties, especially the larger ones, was their undemocratic or even anti-democratic tendencies, and their determination to defend their interests at whatever cost to their principles. There was something defensively medieval about them. Parliament was their fortress and they would pull up its drawbridge when threatened. Not for nothing is its symbol the portcullis.

The Filkin Factor

The most illuminating example of this was their treatment of the former Parliamentary Commissioner for Standards, Elizabeth Filkin, who was dismissed for excellence: she did her job too well to be allowed to stay in it. She was appointed as Parliament's regulator in February 1999, with a remit to investigate allegations of misconduct by MPs. In the normal course of events she would have been asked to serve for a second term when her three-year contract expired; but the normal course of events never happened, nor did the second term. She was fair and thorough and diligent, and upset some powerful political figures of all parties, but principally on the Labour side. I supported her and served alongside her on the Standards and Privileges Committee, which gave me a ringside view of what happened when her inquiries threatened their careers. I like the idea of honest politics; indeed, I was elected on it. The presence of an independent commissioner was the driving force behind the attempt to clean up politics at the time of the Neil Hamilton imbroglio. Elizabeth Filkin found that the House of Commons Commission (the House's ruling body) didn't want a commissioner as independent as she was. Towards the end of her term, in November 2001, she wrote to the Speaker: 'The degree of pressure applied has been quite remarkable. In some cases this has been applied directly by Members, some holding high office. In other cases, it has been applied by unchecked whispering campaigns and hostile briefings ... Insuperable obstacles to independence have now been created by the Commission.'

Elizabeth Filkin was a victim of party politics at its nastiest and most tribal. The whispering campaign arose from friends of high profile Members under her investigation. Most of them were Labour Members, and the whispering was loudest at the Labour end of the Tea Room. She was called 'that bloody woman', 'Mrs Longnose' and 'Cromwell in a skirt'. One MP told another that he thought she was mad. She was by far the sanest person in all that company.

Under pressure from their party and their friends, some Labour Members of the Standards and Privileges Committee, to which she reported, regularly insisted on diluting or contradicting her conclusions. It was the case of John Reid that (in my view) undermined the system. Together with John Maxton MP, he was accused of misusing his parliamentary allowances for campaign purposes in the Scottish elections. The committee ruled that, because the charges were so serious and career-threatening, the burden of proof should be raised from the balance of probabilities to some more exalted level that was never precisely defined. It was a quasi-judicial high jump: we were lifting the bar to a height where no charge could vault over it. The Commissioner felt that John Reid had not been a helpful witness. The committee found only 'misunderstanding'. He was a Secretary of State, and protected by his seniority in a way that a rank-and-file backbencher would not have been.

I should have resigned from Standards and Privileges there and then, but I didn't. I preferred not to break the consensus. It was my worst mistake as an MP. Looking back on it now, I see that as a newcomer to the House of Commons I was too impressed by it as an institution, and revered it rather more than it deserved. I would have done better to enlist from the start where I belonged, as a fully paid-up member of the awkward squad. John Reid, whom I had regarded as a friend, never spoke to me again.

Five of the seven Labour MPs on the committee later received honours or preferments of one sort or another. One became John Reid's Parliamentary Private Secretary. Reward or serendipity? There was no way of knowing; but Alan Williams, a senior committee member beyond the reach of ambition, said, 'Members have to make a choice: they should either be parliamentary private secretary and not on the committee, or vice versa.'[6] Political careerism is a strange affliction. It is like a parliamentary form of Alzheimer's: those who have it don't understand what it is doing to them; but everyone else can see its effects all too clearly.

Elizabeth Filkin's term of office came to an end on 13 February 2002. It was Ash Wednesday, a suitable time for penitence and reflection. MPs debated what Alex Salmond called the 'political assassination' of the Standards Commissioner. They also voted to suspend Keith Vaz from the House for a month for breaches of the MPs' code of conduct. The episode taught me a lesson, in political retirement, that I should have learned while I was still an MP. It is that politics is a feast of fine words, but only the outcomes matter; and the outcomes – however unjust and arbitrary – are determined by party politics. The outcomes in this case were that the winner lost and the loser won: the disgraced Keith Vaz remained in his position as MP for Leicester East, while the vindicated Elizabeth Filkin was ousted from hers as Commissioner for Standards.

9

The Evil That Men Do

Nuremberg and Changi

Two former correspondents were reminiscing under high chandeliers in a wood-panelled room in Germany. I was one and the other was a legend in his country; he was tall, bearded, intense and thoughtful, and had just retired after twenty-two years with *Stern* magazine. We had racketed around together in some of the world's unquiet corners at unquiet times – including the First Gulf War of 1991, where we had both laid siege to the International Press Centre at Dhahran, seeking access to the battlefield. Having the unfair advantage of being British, I was eventually accredited to the 7th Armoured Brigade, the Desert Rats, while he was left languishing at the journalists' wailing wall at the Airport Hotel. He justifiably complained that the British and American armies looked after no one but their own. It was the beginning of the age of rolling news and embedded journalism, and it had not yet dawned on them that news coverage knows no borders.

What made the encounter special was the place and the man. The place was Room 600 of the Justice Building in Nuremberg, where the International Military Tribunal had sat in judgement on twenty-one leading Nazis from November 1945 to October 1946. The man was Niklas Frank, son of Hans Frank, the former Reichsminister and Governor-General of the eastern territories, the self-styled 'King of Poland', who shared the responsibility for the deaths of millions of Jews and Poles during the occupation. He had once gone down on his knees in front of his wife and said, 'Brigit, you will become Queen of Poland.' His crimes caught up with him long before Nuremberg, when he tried to leave his wife for another woman who, because of them, would not have him.

'Do you feel ghosts in this room?' I asked Niklas.

'I feel a bit afraid, as if I had to fight for my life, yes.'

His favoured word for his father was *hündisch*, 'something like a doggish character or slimy character, and Hitler knew quite well what kind of character my father was, so he had the brilliant idea to let him do the dirty work in Poland'.

On 16 October 1946, Hans Frank was one of twelve of Hitler's henchmen to be hanged by British and American executioners in the gymnasium of the prison next to the courthouse. Niklas was only seven years old, but remembered those times vividly and had lived all his life in their shadow. In his extraordinary and most unfilial book about it, he imagined himself playing a personal part in the trial of his father:

> Before I let you die, I have one more meeting with you – in Nuremberg, at the Palace of Justice. Come on in, Father. I have been sitting here for decades waiting for you. I'm seated between His Lordship Judge Lawrence and His Honour United States Judge Birrell. Ever since I was a child I have imagined myself seated here, not next to you in the dock ... He is still the same father I have known from the beginning, a man who turned his heart into a spiders' nest for murderers.[1]

The interview with Niklas Frank was not spontaneous, of course, but choreographed for a television documentary about war crimes. That didn't matter – indeed it was oddly appropriate.

The Nuremberg process was also choreographed – not for television, which was then in its infancy, but for the dominant media of the day, the newspapers and cinema newsreels. For nearly a year, the crimes of the Nazis were set out in print and picture for all to see, especially the German people, so that what was done in their name could not later be denied or mythologized. It was an inspired initiative that could never have happened at the Old Bailey; but for the first time ever, in the former Nazi citadel of Nuremberg, footage of war crimes was played in a court of law.

The strategy worked. There were actually public demonstrations against the three acquittals, including that of Hitler's nominal successor, Admiral of the Fleet Karl Dönitz. (He could not have been convicted of crimes against merchant shipping in the Atlantic, since US Admiral Chester Nimitz had given similar orders to the American fleet in the Pacific. By the same token, the bombing of Coventry was not accounted as a war crime: if it had been, then so was the bombing of Dresden.) After cremation, the bodies of Hitler's lieutenants were burned at Dachau and the ashes were scattered in the fast-flowing River Isar, so that there could be no shrine to them and no place of pilgrimage. The Tribunal was the brainchild of the Americans, who were attached to the idea of legal process, and of the Russians, who knew all there was to know about show trials. Churchill was the odd man out. His preference was to line up the leading Nazis against a wall and have them shot on the spot without trial.

As was his preference, Niklas Frank sat in the presiding judge's chair. In the well of the court the camera turned unnoticed. I was eerily aware that we were not alone, but accompanied by a great crowd of ghosts – not only of his father and Ribbentrop and Goering, but of the judges, the massed ranks of counsel, the photographers with their great cumbersome cameras and the whole parade (or did I mean charade?) of due process. Look at those monochrome photographs now, which peer at us across half a century as if from another age and another planet: nearly all those men (no women then, except interpreters and stenographers) are now dead. The condemned Nazis died first. On an autographed copy of his indictment, Hermann Goering wrote: 'The victor will always be the judge, and the vanquished the accused.'² The American Chief Justice, Harlan Fiske Stone, was of the same opinion: he described the Nuremberg process as 'a high-grade lynching party'.³

The view from Nuremberg was different. The American Chief Prosecutor, Robert Jackson, opening the proceedings on 21 November 1945, called it the first trial in history for crimes against the peace of the world. More than fifty years later its spirit lives on in a world which – perhaps more than at any time since the Third Reich – is also shamed by crimes against humanity and peace and, having lost its moral compass, is less sure how to deal with them. So in a sense, the International Military Tribunal is still in session, and the jury is out – except that there wasn't a jury at Nuremberg – on the justice of it. I found myself playing devil's advocate in the courtroom and attacking the judicial system that Niklas Frank defended. It should have been the other way round. His father, after all, had been the man in the dock and on the scaffold. Mine was a blameless country author – although Adrian Bell kept some odd company in his time, and one of his friends, Henry Williamson of *Tarka the Otter* fame, was interned for fascist sympathies.

'All those cameras in the courtroom – it looked like a show trial, didn't it?'

'No, not from here, not from here. I'm glad I can see pictures of this trial, not just for show effects. I've got all the tapes of my father and it is very good, it's better than only to have seen it in writing ... Every country has a little bit of innocence, but there are always the criminals on top like my father and his bunch and they should be brought to justice.'

'But with the death penalty? Tried for crimes against humanity and then hanged?'

'I'm against the death penalty, but I'm really glad he got the death penalty so at least he experienced the seconds, the hours, the days and nights before death which he brought to millions of people.'

'It was victor's justice, wasn't it?'

'That's a philosophical question and I don't want to deal with it. They did such horrendous criminal things that they had to be punished.'

It was a curious legacy of the Second World War that those who were close to its criminals – whether by ties of blood or physical proximity – strongly opposed the death penalty in principle, except as it applied to those men and the crimes they committed at that time.

A no less compelling witness was Emil Salem, a robust Lancastrian of Spanish origin, who came to see me in Knutsford during my time as an MP. He bore more than a passing resemblance to Telly Savalas, and was also an angler, which helped him. The angling led him to calm waters, which were the best relief for all that life had thrown at him. Emil had once been active in politics as an alderman and had nearly stood for Parliament as Liberal candidate for Clitheroe. He stepped down only when he found that, for personal reasons, he couldn't find easy answers to questions about capital punishment, which was at that time a defining political issue. Now in his late seventies, he wanted me to help him harness the concerns of pensioners to a new political movement. I discouraged him gently (most new political movements end in tears), but I found his personal story deeply moving. At the end of the Second World War, as a nineteen-year-old conscript, he had been posted with the 2nd Battalion of the Parachute Regiment to Singapore. The soldiers' duties had included assisting the executioners of former Japanese camp commandants and other war criminals at Changi Jail. He had personally helped to place the black bags over their heads and escorted eleven of them up a ramp to the execution chamber, where a Dutch hangman pulled the lever that opened the trapdoor under their feet. They were then left to hang for thirteen minutes. Those experiences had marked him for life, and he still had nightmares about them.

He also remembered, as a schoolboy, singing a song of the

British Expeditionary Force sent to Abyssinia following the Italians' use of mustard gas against the native population in 1935 – an exploit forgotten by just about everyone except for Emil Salem. I love the company of old soldiers, whose minds are living history books; and he had the most remarkable memory of anyone I knew. He wrote plaintively, 'No one believes it':

> Will you come to Abyssinia, will you come?
> Will you bring your ammunition and your gun?
> Mussolini will be there, shooting peanuts in the air.
> Will you come to Abyssinia, will you come?

His experience of Changi Jail, which lacked the good cheer of soldiers' songs, was altogether more sombre: 'It was a terrible job. No one should have to do it and of course we weren't prepared. We never expected to be involved in this sort of thing. There were two Dutch hangmen and the rest were soldiers; and when our names went up on the board as being on duty the next day it was a terrible feeling, you didn't sleep at night.' Other paratroopers, who couldn't bear to look at the rosters, asked Emil to go to the board and tell them what their duties were next morning. It was summary justice with no due process at all. We have long forgotten – perhaps we have preferred to forget – those who opened the trapdoor in our name.

The Hague

After the tribunals in Changi and Nuremberg, the ideas of international justice and redress for crimes against humanity disappeared for fifty years into the deep freeze of the Cold War. When the Cold War was over and Yugoslavia disintegrated, those ideas were revived as a result of the barbarities of the wars in Bosnia and Croatia, and later Rwanda and Sierra Leone, and the immunity of those responsible from prosecution in their national courts. They were both civil wars and wars of international aggression, fought without codes of honour; one side's war criminal was another's war hero. To call these barbarities medieval, as commentators tended to, was a quite unwarranted slur on the Middle Ages. From Vukovar in Croatia, to Ahmici in Bosnia, I had been a witness to the effects of war crimes that I had never expected to see in my continent and in my lifetime. So I should have welcomed the establishment of the International Criminal Court in The Hague to seek out and punish those responsible. Nuremberg was its inspiration. It was the direct descendant of the process there, but without the ultimate sanction of the death penalty.

And yet ... it is the way of the world that politics comes first and justice second. The Hague Tribunal had American impetus behind it and is still sometimes referred to as Madeleine Albright's court (she was the US Secretary of State at the time). It was political at birth, established in the spring of 1993, at the darkest hour of the Bosnian war, when negotiation had failed and the Security Council was unwilling to authorize the sort of effective intervention against the Serbs which – two and a half years and tens of thousands of deaths later – eventually brought the conflict to an end. So it proposed a series of half-measures substituting for action: economic sanctions, no-fly zones (an offence against literacy as well as strategy – they should have been called no-flight zones) and, most notoriously, the so-called 'safe areas', which were a murderous illusion and a threat to the people they were supposed to protect. The International Criminal Tribunal belonged to the gesture politics of the time. It floated the idea that the war criminals of ex-Yugoslavia would eventually be brought to trial in a brave new world – no one knew when or how, but it left the politicians with an afterglow of satisfaction. Even one of the court's champions, Geoffrey Robertson QC, was candid about its somewhat disreputable origins: 'The Hague Tribunal worked rather well as a publicity stunt, and that was what the diplomats thought it would be, all that they thought it would be, back in 1993.' As time went by, it outgrew its parentage and took on a life of its own.

The court made a faltering start. It trapped the little fish while the two big fish swam free. Its prime suspects, Radovan Karadzic and Ratko Mladic, eluded it and gained prestige among the Bosnian Serbs by doing so. The mediocre Karadzic could thank Nato's bungled plans to arrest him, twice betrayed by a French informer, for turning him almost into a figure of legend. The borderland between Bosnia and Montenegro was his Sherwood Forest. The court tried and convicted the foot soldiers and functionaries, like two of the executioners at Srebrenica (one of them actually a Croat), who argued that, if they had not carried out their orders, they would themselves have been shot by the Bosnian Serb Army in which they served. They were probably right about that. Not for four years did any of the principal decision-makers face trial. The first to do so was Tihomir Blaskic, commander of the Bosnian Croat forces in the Lasva Valley during the brutal side-war between Croats and Muslims in 1993 and 1994. He was accused of complicity in the Ahmici massacre of April 1993, in which two hundred Muslims were shot trying to escape or burned alive in their homes. I was the BBC correspondent in central Bosnia at the time, and the videotape of my report from Ahmici was played as evidence on the court's TV screens: The Hague, like Nuremberg, was wired for the images of war. The report had a certain impact at the time, and there were even those who believed that it was partly responsible for the establishment of the Hague Tribunal.

I appeared before the court as a witness – on behalf of Blaskic. This too was controversial. Many journalists were asked to testify, and very few chose to do so, on the grounds that they would be compromised and endangered. My view was different: I believed that Blaskic was innocent and that I should try to help him. I had been around war-zone psychopaths long enough to know one when I saw one. The quiet and soldierly Blaskic wasn't the type. His lawyer Russell Hayman asked me, 'Did you ever hear him express intolerant, racist or discriminatory views towards persons of Muslim origin?'

'No, sir, I never did. I always regarded him as a correct military man.'

I explained the chaos in the valley at the time, the plight of the outnumbered Croats, the roles of the Fedayeen on one side and the gangs of paramilitaries on the other, and the absence of a regular chain of command. When the session was over, I crossed the floor to the dock, shook Blaskic by the hand and wished him all the luck that he needed, which was more than he had. I believed then, and still believe, that the death squad responsible for the Ahmici massacre was operating on someone else's orders. Evidence later came to light, after President Tudjman's death and in his palace, that the instructions came directly from Zagreb and bypassed the Croats' commander in the field. It didn't save him from what amounted to a life sentence. He joined the crowded ranks of the war's victims.

My personal experience of the Tribunal disturbed me deeply, and I did myself no favours in the eyes of its prosecutors by expressing my criticisms in a Croatian magazine. The court's procedures were painfully slow. Blaskic had been in prison for nearly three years before his trial began; and I worked out that, had he been acquitted, the judges' coffee breaks alone would have cost him eleven days of his freedom. They were not noted for working all the hours that God gave. More serious was the collegiality of the judges and prosecutors; they were part of the same establishment and housed under the same roof. Defence lawyers were outsiders, coming in on trial days only and sharing a single room. They complained from the outset (the Tadic case in 1996) that the scales of justice were weighted against them, especially through the admission of hearsay evidence from anonymous witnesses. The South African Judge, Richard Goldstone, a good man and the Tribunal's first Chief Prosecutor, was well aware of the handicaps under which the accused tried to prove their innocence. He told his staff that he would rather lose all the cases than win one with a justifiable allegation of unfairness; but at The Hague there was no equivalent of Nuremberg's Admiral Dönitz. We waited in vain for the first high-profile acquittal.

We are still waiting. The court had a political parentage. It was probationary and expensive; and to justify the cost it appeared to feed on a diet of convictions.

Its supreme test was the trial of Slobodan Milosevic, which opened in February 2002 – a heady blend of courtroom drama, politics and pantomime. The court did Milosevic a favour by extraditing him. Back in Belgrade he would have been tried for embezzlement; but in the court that he didn't recognize he could strut on the world stage again, through television, as the defender and champion of his people. It played well for him on the nightly newscasts at home. The verdict would be fateful not only for the accused, the first former head of state to come before it, but also for the Tribunal and its reputation. Courts try cases, but cases also try courts. Geoffrey Robertson QC noted that Milosevic, like Goering before him, could not resist defending himself in a court that he claimed was unlawful: 'Unlike Charles I, who preserved his martyr status by resisting all temptation to enter the forensic fray, Mr Milosevic's participation in the proceedings has served, ironically, to legitimise them.'[4]

My mind went back some years to long conversations with my friend – a loose term, depending on how friendship is defined – Zeljko Raznjatovic, also known as Arkan, a war criminal who was indicted by the Tribunal until someone else got to him first. In 2000 he met summary justice through an assassin's bullet outside the Intercontinental Hotel in Belgrade. During the Croatian and Bosnian wars I sought him out, sometimes in his civilian headquarters, which was an ice-cream parlour outside the gates of the Red Star Football Club. It is difficult to conduct a blood-curdling interview with a warlord eating a vanilla ice cream. He knew that: it was part of his cover as an all-round regular guy and family man. He even offered me Red Star membership, but he died before the membership card could reach me.

Arkan hated the Yugoslav Communists. 'They see the sky red,' he told me, 'they see the earth red. It's "comrade major" this and "comrade captain" that. They have no motivation.' Then he whipped out an ornate silver cross on a chain from beneath his uniform to show his credentials as an Orthodox Christian. He insisted on having his volunteers baptized. He spoke ill of Milosevic, yet did the dictator's dirty work for him. He led his paramilitary tigers in murderous expeditions – he saw them as 'actions' – near Vukovar, in Croatia, and Zvornik and Bjeljina, in Bosnia. The licence to kill came from the Serbian leadership, which was essentially a one-man band. Although Milosevic was head of state, it would be hard to tie him to specific crimes committed at some distance from Belgrade, and especially hard in the absence of written orders and key witnesses. Most of the mass murders, until Srebrenica, were carried out by irregulars. The speculation in Belgrade was that Arkan was assassinated because he knew too much, and would himself have been a compelling witness. A little knowledge was a dangerous thing in a city bristling with guns.

There was also the troublesome issue of victors' justice – the 'high-grade lynch mob'. Whoever wins the war gets to write not only the history, but these days the indictments as well. The Tribunal was the creation of the Western democracies, whose enforcement agency was NATO.

Milosevic was accused, with other named individuals, of participation in joint criminal enterprises in Croatia, Bosnia and Kosovo; but NATO's planners and pilots, the bombers of bridges and TV stations in Serbia and Kosovo, were ruled by the court to be outside its jurisdiction. The targeting of civilians is forbidden under the Geneva Conventions. The bridges had both civilian and military uses; but the TV station in Belgrade was a civilian installation and the attack on it bore the marks of a war crime. The argument that it was bombed because it was broadcasting lies hardly stands up to scrutiny. The justification for NATO's actions amounted, in the last resort, to a plea of proportionality: it committed only little war crimes, while the Serbs committed big ones.

Just as the Tribunal at The Hague drew on the precedent of Nuremberg, so it was itself the model for the International Criminal Court voted into being by the UN's Rome Conference in 1998. It was a flawed model. I have seen enough of war crimes around the world to support a system of international justice to deal with them, but not this system. While I was still an MP I expressed doubts about the enabling legislation, and my last speech in the House of Commons was a defence of the rights of accused war criminals. If an Independent couldn't make that case, who could? I even received a note of appreciation from Lord Lamont, the former Conservative cabinet minister, who had supposed that I was referring to the Chilean dictator, General Pinochet. I wasn't, but the same rule applies: justice isn't a popularity contest and has nothing to do with headlines. It is the hard cases – Milosevic and Pinochet among them – that test its quality. In a civilized society it is better that a suspect should walk free for lack of evidence, than that he be convicted on grounds of mere notoriety. Hostile headlines do not amount to evidence.

Strangest of all was the attitude of the Americans. They had been the driving force behind the tribunals at Nuremberg and The Hague; but, invited to accept the International Criminal Court, they first hesitated and then walked away. The Clinton Administration signed on reluctantly, but had second thoughts under the pressure of an election campaign and refused to submit the measure for Senate ratification. The Bush Administration took the view that it was hostile to American interests. Senator Jesse Helms of North Carolina called it the International Kangaroo Court. Senator Larry Craig of Idaho saw it as a rogue court. 'You run the risk,' he told me, 'of a rogue prosecutor some day going down a road where our nation would not want to go.' That meant a court that might prosecute Americans, and especially their soldiers serving overseas. They saw themselves as prosecutors but never as defendants. In the unlikely event that Americans committed war crimes, they would be tried in the American way by American courts. Lieutenant Calley, responsible for the My Lai massacre in Vietnam, became a kind of celebrity, and to some a national hero.

11 September

The Americans' hostility to the court was not moderated by the events of 11 September 2001 – the most devastating attack on the continental United States since the British soldiers of the East Essex Regiment, and a few others, defeated the Americans at Bladensburg in 1814, and went on to burn down the White House. The destruction of the World Trade Center in New York was planned in a foreign country and executed by the citizens of many foreign countries. It was a crime committed on a global scale with global accomplices, but it did not convince the Americans of the case for a global court. Rather the reverse. They would retreat into fortress America and do it their way: extradite suspects by special forces snatch squads, cage them and chain them, detain them without trial or bring them before military tribunals, apply the death penalty if they wished and even plan and launch two wars of revenge. It was Rambo justice, Rambo politics and ultimately Rambo warfare. It had no place in a civilized society.

In the never-ending dialogue between the government and the governed, the raucous American media free-for-all where no opinion goes unanswered, the opposition was either muted or found no one to give it a platform. The TV networks echoed the White House line. To a visitor to the United States at the time, the silencing of democratic debate was almost as shocking as the scene at Ground Zero itself. It was like being in a country at war – indeed, it saw itself as a country at war – in which dissent was counted as treason. The civil libertarians had fled from the scene, on the grounds that the defence of those suspected of terrorism was a campaign too far. In the home of the brave and the land of the free, after 11 September 2001, their rights did not seem to the press and the public to be an issue of much consequence. The country that had brought due process to Nuremberg did not extend it to the prisoners of Camp X-Ray in Guantanamo Bay. One of them was a child of thirteen and another was a man who claimed to be a hundred and five years old and had no idea why he had been transported halfway round the world. (He was later released.) Senator Craig, having visited the prisoners, saw them as enjoying the benefits of America's hospitality. 'They're living in open, airy situations,' he said, 'they're being well cared for because we are a humane nation.' Again it was politics first and justice second. I was based for twelve years in the United States as the BBC's correspondent and found it a fascinating experience, with every day a fresh source of astonishment; but I also learned what it was like to be divided by a common language. I thought that common values would go with it, but they didn't. Of all the ninety countries I worked in, it seemed to me, with the possible exception of Equatorial Guinea, to be the most alien.

The spirit of 'America first' prevailed even in academia, where every thesis will usually find its antithesis. Not this time: the campus at Yale was almost as festooned with the Stars and Stripes as the streets of Manhattan; but there was one witness with an alternative view and a special right to be heard. Dr Robin Theurkauf, a lecturer in international law, was taking her weekly politics seminar into issues arising from the detention of al-Qaeda suspects in Cuba. She explained the Administration's policy of denying them prisoner-of-war status on the grounds that they were 'illegal combatants', and asked her students to refer to the Geneva Conventions and think this through for themselves. What they didn't know, because she didn't tell them, was that she was herself a victim of the attacks on 11 September. Her husband Tom, the director of a bank, had died in his office in one of the towers of the World Trade Center. She was not only an expert on the International Criminal Court; she was also a new widow with three young sons. 'Ironic, isn't it?' she said, and her Grace Kelly features melted into a slow, sad smile. Her liberal and now unfashionable views had not changed as a result of her personal tragedy. She set them out firmly and quietly:

> I have always felt that if we are going to have a peaceful world, we need to individualize criminal actions in the international setting. I have always believed that the death penalty is inappropriate under any circumstances, and I still believe that. The idea that the United States would try any of the perpetrators of this crime on capital charges in my name offends me. I have lost an awful lot in this disaster, and I don't feel that I need to give up any of my humanity in addition.

Our civil societies do not respond well to attacks on them. We intern without trial, we rush draconian measures through fearful legislatures, we stigmatize groups of people whose loyalty we suspect. When we go to war, we establish one set of rules for our troops and another for the enemy's. In March 2003 we saw nothing wrong with showing television images of Iraqi casualties and prisoners, yet when al-Jazeera television did the same thing to ours, we responded with cries of outrage and accused them of breaches of the Geneva Conventions. Our attitude to the Conventions, like our attitude to the UN, is to respect them when it suits us and to defy them when it doesn't.

Crimes against humanity did not end with the Second World War. They are still with us, taking new and terrible forms as war crimes and acts of terrorism; but our way of dealing with them – indeed, whether we deal with them at all – appears to depend on the identity of the victims. Our concept of global justice, as enshrined in the International Criminal Court, is politically blinkered (it exempts the Americans, for instance) and has probably regressed since Nuremberg, when the Americans were on the side of the idealists. I am not convinced that half a system of justice is better than none, though Geoffrey Robertson QC disagrees: 'No politician from Russia is going to be accused of war crimes in Chechnya, just as no American general is ever going to be accused of letting his men run amok in Iraq. My view is that justice is more important in the world than diplomacy and appeasement, and I don't mind making a start somewhere.'

The strong element of due process in Nuremberg, which produced three historic acquittals despite Russian objections, has been weakened in The Hague. The zeal of the prosecutors drives the process. Anti-terrorist legislation, which is usually passed in haste and repented at leisure, also challenges the principle of due process. Terrorism brings out the worst in us, provoking us to blind retaliation. The mark of a civilized society is to distinguish between justice and vengeance. If our response to atrocities committed against us is to round up such suspects as we can find, of all ages and origins, deny them their rights, humiliate them, manacle them in cages, and haul them before military tribunals dispensing death and revenge, then we shall have sacrificed the values we are trying to defend. And we shall emerge as the losers – twice over.

10

Journalism for Better ...

Soldiers and Scapegoats

In a book about the Bosnian war, I used the phrase 'the journalism of attachment' to chart the way in which news reporting changed and developed. It wasn't a doctrine; it was a description. Critics seized on it as a heresy, which it wasn't. 'Martin Bell is talking nonsense and he knows it,' declared my colleague John Simpson rather sniffily in one of his newspaper columns. I was talking sense and I hope that he now knows it. It can also be defined as a journalism that cares as well as knows. It is a practical and humane code of practice that has gained ground through the turbulent times at the end of one century and the beginning of another, when the old ways of doing things proved inadequate. If I played a part in that change, I have no apologies to offer – and no regrets.

I saw my first herd of journalists when I was a young soldier with the Suffolk Regiment in Cyprus in the summer of 1958.

'You're a college boy, aren't you?' accused the sergeant of the 1st Battalion's training company on the day when I signed on.

'Yes, sergeant, I suppose I am,' I admitted. I had left a middle-ranking public school and failed my officer-selection test; but I didn't talk posh, and my only objective was to let the days roll by without being noticed by the sergeant. No chance.

'I can always spot 'em,' he said triumphantly.

From that point on I was marked out for extra fatigues and guard duties. Window-cleaning and stone-painting were my specialities; but since literacy was in short supply in the battalion, I also edited the regimental magazine and became a lance corporal in the intelligence section, issuing maps, keeping log books and obtaining work permits for the Indian camp-followers, the char-wallahs and dhobi-wallahs (tea and laundry, to the uninitiated). From time to time I put down my pen, picked up a gun and put in a bit of active service. It was known to the old sweats as 'getting your knees brown'. I was attached to a rifle company on an operation in a Turkish suburb of Nicosia. Cyprus was still a British possession, and I suppose I was part of the colonial jackboot, although I never saw it like that or gave it much thought. My letters home, which my mother kept in a shoe box, were so politically mindless that I destroyed them many years later; I was not old enough to have earned the right to such opinions. It was a time of violence between Greeks and Turks, with the steady Suffolks positioned in the middle (the Scots and Irish were banished to the Troodos Mountains). Our orders were to search the suburb's houses for anything that could be used as an offensive weapon. The resulting haul, ranging from crowbars to carving knives, was set out on trestle tables for the inspection of the international press. I didn't know it at the time, but this was my first glimpse of a photo opportunity.

The journalists looked a sophisticated bunch to my impressionable eye – almost like a patrol of their own – uniformly kitted out with eyeshades, dark glasses, safari suits, suede shoes, cameras and notebooks. They seemed at ease with each other and with the army. Even the sergeant was treating them with respect, which was not his natural manner. They included such veterans as Donald Wise of the *Mirror* (and formerly of the Suffolk Regiment) and John Osman of the *Telegraph*. I supposed that, summoned by the army, they had hoisted themselves from the bar stools of the Ledra Palace Hotel, their home-from-home, which was out of bounds to us mere other ranks. In due course they would slide back into its air-conditioned luxury, to file their reports with a telephone in one hand and an ice-cold gin and tonic in the other. I, on the other hand, would clean my dusty rifle and retreat to a windblown tent in the camp on the airport road, a cookhouse meal in a mess tin and a Keo beer if I was lucky; then, after scouring the mess tin, I would do the accounts for the corporals' mess, of which I had been made secretary because it was rumoured that I knew how to add up. That was the moment when I decided that, if the dreams of lance corporals ever came true, what I wanted more than anything else was to be a foreign correspondent when my time as a soldier was over.

Eight years later, and after various rites of passage, I became one. Not only that, but my early colleagues included John Osman, last seen in Cyprus, who had migrated to the BBC. We worked together on BBC2's *Newsroom*, which was the first British experiment in a half-hour news programme, but was broadcast around midnight to an audience so small that it would have been cheaper to close the transmitter and bring them in by bus. From John and the other old hands, Christopher Serpell and John Timpson, I learned a lot that I needed to learn; and I studied the tradecraft of a recruit from Fleet Street, Tom Mangold, a serious foot-in-the-door artist who was strong in the areas, such as crime reporting, where I knew that I was weak. Mangold's telephone technique charmed birds off trees and was regularly a performance worth an Oscar. News was a wide waterfront in those days. There was little specialization, and much scrambling after the big story. Great opportunities awaited those who were first at the airport, or fastest out of the door. Like many reporters, I was torn between a fear of being found out, and the firm belief that the scoop of a lifetime was waiting just around the corner.

We were aware of working in a great tradition. The BBC had an unrivalled reputation, as for most of the time it still has, especially since it has recovered its confidence under the piratical leadership of Greg Dyke. Wherever you were in the world, correspondents of all nationalities – even the Czechs and their spymasters, the Russians – would fall silent as the strains of *Lillibullero*, an Ulster Protestant marching tune, announced the news from London. It was delivered in the tones of the officer class and had a distinctive character – cautious, Olympian, even-handed, passionless, and strangely remote – as if it were reporting events on another planet. I had neither the experience nor the slightest wish to challenge the prevailing culture; but I did wonder why, on joining, I had been required to sign the Official Secrets Act. Why did the BBC's Paris office share the same staircase as the MI6 office, which was disguised as a military charity? Which of my colleagues were moonlighting as spies? Why did the BBC have an intelligence officer on its staff, serving as its representative in a sensitive part of the world, and why did he receive the MBE for it? I also noted that a diplomatic correspondent who had been thought by the Foreign Office to be 'unhelpful' was swiftly removed and exiled to the Asian equivalent of the Patagonia bureau. Not for nothing was the in-house magazine known to us as 'Pravda'. The Corporation had a Kremlinesque way of dealing with those of its staff who stepped out of line.

The most notable example, not lost on any of us, was that of Frederick Forsyth, later to make a name for himself as a thriller writer. We were contemporaries from East Anglia, we had joined at the same time, and had once covered a rail crash together in Kentish Town – each on opposite sides of the train, neither of us knowing that the other was there. His career track proved to be faster than mine. By June 1967 he was the Assistant Diplomatic Correspondent. The rest of us were away in the Middle East reporting the Six Days' War, when the Eastern region of Nigeria declared its independence as Biafra, making civil war there inevitable. Freddie was sent to cover the Biafrans' side of it. They had a charismatic leader, Colonel Odemugwu Ojukwu, and a strong case – their people, the Ibos, had been victims of genocide and what is now called ethnic cleansing, in Northern Nigeria. All that Freddie Forsyth did, to the best of his considerable ability, was to report their claims, the progress of the war and the effect of the subsequent blockade on the enclave and its people. Britain was by no means neutral, but a provider of armoured vehicles and fighter pilots to the Federal Nigerian Government. The South Africans were also involved on the Nigerian side, even though it was the heyday of apartheid. One of them was a pilot whose name was Bond – we knew him as Boozy Bonzo Bond – whose personal fuel was half a bottle of gin before take-off, in an ancient DC3 which he flew out of Makurdi as a bomber; the bomb bay was the port-side passenger door. I like being flown by old pilots and don't even mind being flown by drunken ones, since their experience tends to make up for their insobriety. The Biafran war may be little remembered today, but it was a burning moral issue at the time, and a bigger issue in the United Kingdom than even Vietnam.

The British High Commissioner in Lagos was much offended that the BBC, the national broadcaster, was not just reporting the war from both sides of the lines, but doing rather better from Biafra, where its correspondent enjoyed easier access than Angus McDermid in Lagos, who had to deal with the Byzantine Nigerian censorship. The Foreign Office protested to the BBC; and in short order Frederick Forsyth was scapegoated. He wasn't exactly court-martialled and paraded in front of the rest us in a hollow square – but he was withdrawn from the war zone, reduced in rank and returned to the pool of general reporters to which I belonged at the time. To his great credit he resigned. In the weeks following, he retreated to a friend's flat in Primrose Hill and wrote his first book, *The Day of the Jackal*, drawing in part on the reminiscences of French and Belgian mercenaries in Biafra. He later found his way back there and served, almost to the end and at great risk, as a captain in Ojukwu's army. The opening chapter of his second book, *The Dogs of War*, is the most vivid account in fact or fiction of the last days of Biafra.

We were on opposite sides both in the war and the reporting of it. I was advancing with an armoured column of the Federal

Nigerian Army just after the fall of the Biafran capital, Enugu. The Nigerian civil war was a bush war that followed African rules, not those of an army staff college. The armoured vehicles rumbled out of town with a battalion of infantry beside and behind them, until they ran into a fire-fight at a left-handed bend two miles down the road. I have forgotten so much across the years, but not that bend in the road. Inevitably the column took casualties. My cameraman was Nigerian, and I was the only white face among many hundreds of black ones. I should at least have blacked up beforehand, and I reproached myself for the failure of my fieldcraft; but it also set me thinking about different types of courage. The sort it takes to walk into an ambush is physical courage. You either have it or you don't; it is not a moral quality. The sort that Freddie had shown, in his principled resignation and refusal to be silenced, was the much rarer quality of moral courage. We both survived, one of us still with a BBC salary and the other one without, but he came out of it with rather more credit than I did; and we both did better than the column's commander, Brigadier Yakubu Danjuma of the Nigerian army, who was later accused of treason and executed.

Crises of Conscience

I was only twenty-nine at the time with a lot to learn; but the Forsyth saga also had me wondering how independent and even-handed the BBC really was. It had not been neutral between the Nigerian government and the Biafran rebels, but on issues where the Foreign Office took less of an interest it followed a policy of the most determined even-handedness. 'The ruling junta blames the leftists, but the leftists say it is all the fault of the junta' was a typically undistinguished example for which I was personally to blame. It came from a report from El Salvador in 1982, but I could have written it at just about any time in any place, and probably did. The basic formula was: 'On the one hand this . . . on the other hand that . . . Only time will tell.' Try applying that to Nazi Germany: 'On the one hand the regime killed millions of Jews, on the other it built the autobahns and made the trains run on time . . . Whatever else you could say about him, Herr Hitler certainly made an impact.' The BBC's imperative was to take no risks and make no waves, but to find – and even construct, if necessary – an expedient fence to sit on. The mind-set was one of extreme detachment, taking its text from a speech by Shakespeare's Romeo, 'I'll be a candle-holder and look on.' This was a theory of bystanders' journalism – being on stage and shedding light on events, but not affecting them or being affected by them.

It was nonsense. I went along with it but was beginning to grow sceptical. The new technology of television had a dynamic of its own that was changing the landscape in which we operated: journalists not only reflected but affected the events they were reporting. From time to time things happened that made me doubt the BBC's doctrine of the journalist's *apartness*. One of these was the show trial of British mercenaries in Angola in 1976. The leader of the group was the self-styled 'Colonel Callan', a Greek Cypriot of British nationality from Camden Town. Their capture, while fighting for Holden Roberto's guerrilla army in the north of the country, was a propaganda coup for Angola's new Marxist government. International observers and journalists were invited to the 'people's court' in Luanda. 'Callan' was represented by British and Angolan lawyers, and his sister flew there to try to save him. I befriended her, not just for professional reasons, but because she was a really brave and sympathetic woman; we went for walks together, and I did what I could to keep up her courage and spirits. I found out things about her during her time in Angola that I didn't broadcast, for fear of their effect on her and her family. It had taken a hell of a long time, but perhaps I was beginning to behave like a human being rather than a cog in the news machine.

The outcome of the trial was inevitable. Her brother was

found guilty and executed. His body was returned to England. She called me and invited me, not as a reporter but as a friend, to the funeral service at the Greek Orthodox Cathedral in Camden Town and the private burial afterwards. The press were desperate to find out the times and places, but I did not even tell my news desk at the BBC. I did not attend the funeral myself, which I should have done; I gave some lame excuse about a dentist's appointment. I was so brainwashed by notions of neutrality that I felt that to have paid my respects, even privately, to a mercenary victim of the Angolan war would somehow have compromised my neutrality as a BBC reporter. This was absurd. There was no reason why it should matter to anyone else, but it became an important symbolic issue to me.

Another crisis of conscience arose from the war in El Salvador. Again it was retrospective and about a funeral. In March 1980, the country's respected Roman Catholic Archbishop, Oscar Romero, was murdered by gunmen as he worshipped in a chapel – the most prominent of hundreds of victims of the notorious death squads. The funeral was held on the steps of the great unfinished brick-and-concrete cathedral in San Salvador. Many groups attended, including bishops and archbishops from throughout Latin America, devout Salvadorans holding reeds, which were the symbols of mourning, and leftist demonstrators bearing rifles, which they made a token attempt to conceal in cardboard boxes. At the request of the Church, the army and police stayed away, and such crowd control as existed was the responsibility of the Boy Scouts. An hour into the service, while the Archbishop of Mexico was halfway though the eulogy, there was a loud explosion from the far side of the square. Its origin was never discovered, but it led to exchanges of gunfire across the square and a stampede by the people to reach the sanctuary of the cathedral.

The iron gates, which opened outwards at the bottom of the steps, were shut fast by the pressure of the crowd. Those at the front included the elderly and infirm, who had been there since dawn for the best view of the service. Twenty of them died in the panic, trampled underfoot and suffocated. The press, like the bishops, were on the cathedral steps on the safe side of the railings. Some attempts were made to lift people over, and I remember having joined in briefly but not nearly enough. I should have dropped what I was doing completely and become a full-time rescue worker – a human being first and a journalist second, if at all; but I didn't. The BBC habit of detachment died hard. It seemed that funerals brought out the worst in me.

The old way of doing things in journalism died its death, unlamented, in the course of the Balkan wars. There were four of those wars – Slovenia, Croatia, Bosnia and Kosovo – and almost a fifth in Macedonia. Slovenia's war, provoked by its declaration of independence in June 1991, lasted only twelve days with relatively light casualties. It included an attack on the inaptly named Highway of Brotherhood and Unity, where the Slovenes ambushed and blocked a federal army column trying to flee to the relative safety of the garrison in Zagreb. When the fighting died down, we made our way to it across the fields, and sought permission to approach the column from the direction of the roadblock. I waved a Union Jack, which I happened to have with me, as a symbol of neutrality and non-belligerence. The Serbian colonel commanding the column was nervous, but allowed us through and told us of his predicament, which was desperate: no way forward, no way back, and a badly wounded soldier awaiting treatment in an armoured ambulance. Instead of completing the report, thanking the colonel and walking away, which I would have done in the old days, I suggested that we took the wounded man out with us. The colonel agreed. So we backed the camera car up to the embankment, and drove to the clinic in the nearest village, where the Slovenes looked after him as if he had been one of their own. It should be a matter of honour in a war zone – and it was in Slovenia, which was the Slovenes' unique distinction in these wars – to treat wounded soldiers as if they were civilians. The Croats, Serbs and Bosnian Muslims didn't do that, except in rare cases, but would rather have sacrificed their own than help their enemies.

The next morning in the capital, Ljubljana, I received a 'feeling-of-the-meeting' call from the foreign editor, John Mahoney. 'Feeling-of-the-meeting' calls are always bad news for reporters in the field. I thought I was about to be reproached for getting too involved in the war, but that wasn't it. I could have liberated the entire Yugoslav army for all they cared.

'Nice piece that last night,' said John, 'but the feeling of the meeting was that the shot of you waving the flag was over the top.'

'How do you mean exactly, John – over the top?'

'Well, it looked out of place, as if you were leading a loyalist parade in Belfast.'

'It kept us alive,' I said, 'and, if you don't mind, I'll do it again if I have to.'

It always worked to play the safety card. The BBC, for all its faults, was sound on safety. Its Head of Newsgathering, Chris Cramer, had been held as a hostage in the siege of the Iranian Embassy in London in 1980. It broke his nerve and left him deeply suspicious of macho journalism.

I don't know whether I qualified as a macho journalist. In his terms I probably did, but I could also make a convincing show of cowardice. I played the safety card again a month later, in the no-man's-land of the bridge at Kostajnica over the River Una between Bosnia and Croatia, with the Serbs on one side and the Croats on the other. It worked for us there as well. After all, the Croats went over the top with their own flags all the time: the war there was initially *about* flags – Croatian flags being hoisted at police stations in predominantly Serbian villages. A British flag, being strenuously waved by a man in a white suit, didn't strike them as being so very much out of the ordinary; and when I was back in London I bought another one, from a tourist kiosk in Piccadilly Circus, just in case I needed it. *Just like the American Express card*, I thought: *don't leave home without it.*

Above all it was the Bosnian war that made the old ways of working unthinkable. Whether we liked it or not – and we often did not – we were in the thick of things. The usual war-zone sanctuaries were not available. The only escape in Sarajevo was to the Holiday Inn, which was itself half-ruined and besieged. We helped where we could, carried parcels and messages, and in emergencies applied field dressings to the wounded. The Reuters bureau chief Kurt Schork had a moral force and personality that made him our natural leader and conscience-in-residence. He was killed in Sierra Leone in May 2000. In due course the airport road in Sarajevo became the Ulica Kurta Schorka in his honour. Being gunned down in a tin-pot African ambush was one hell of a price to pay for having a road named after him.

It was Kurt who demanded that the UN fulfil its mandate, and who led the outcry when the UN spokesman, the Canadian Colonel Barry Frewer, claimed that Sarajevo was not besieged but 'tactically encircled'. It was Jonathan Randall, the scholarly correspondent of the *Washington Post*, who, after another UN capitulation, pursued its special envoy, Yasushi Akashi, down the staircase of the Presidency with cries of 'Shame on you, shame on you'; and when the Bosnian deputy prime minister, Hakija Turajlic, was shot dead by the Serbs in the back of a French armoured vehicle, it was a French radio reporter, Paul Marchand, who concluded his report with just the same words, 'La honte, la honte.' All of this was a long way from the practice of balanced, steady and even-handed on-the-one-hand-on-the-other-hand journalism in which I had been schooled; but the old rules didn't apply any more: the times had changed, we had changed with them and for perhaps the first time in our lives we knew that we were right.

Was there an agenda? Maybe in some cases there was, coupled with an unwillingness to seek out the Serbs and understand them. I tried more than most; but Kurt Schork met their commander General Mladic only once, at Sarajevo airport, and when he did I had to save him from physical assault. He had an unusual descriptive style for an agency man – 'The captain smiled, and the sunlight glinted on his golden beard' – which Reuters tried to moderate through the bureaucratic filter of its Belgrade bureau; but his courage and determination to establish the facts lay at the heart of the Reuters tradition. The UN's daily press briefings became something of a courtroom drama, with Kurt Schork leading for the prosecution; and those who harried the UN for its failures were, with the exception of the gifted Joel Brand of *The Times*, not newcomers to journalism but veteran foreign correspondents. We had been around for a while.

Bystanders No More

Two things had changed between the old journalism and the new. One was that we were no longer bystanders but players, and not all the time marginal players, in the conduct of armed conflict. The war of words and clash of arms ran parallel to each other and interacted. That is why television especially was blocked, manipulated, threatened and cajoled to an unprecedented extent. In the absence of the diplomats, whose finest hour this was not, it was how the political and military leaders on all sides made their case to the outside world. It was sometimes their only channel of communication; and in the end, it was how the Bosnian government lost the war but won the peace, although not on the terms that it wanted.

The other change was that, over the years, and not by design but by evolution, we had humanized the reporting of warfare. When I started in Vietnam and Israel in 1967, I had studied the practice of others and supposed it was about strategies, military formations and weapons systems. When I finished, in Bosnia in 1996, it was about people – the people who wage war and the people who suffer from war, who are often the same people. It saw soldiers not as numbers in an order of battle but as human beings with the hopes and fears that anyone else would have when staring at death down the barrel of a gun; and whoever believes soldiers are fearless doesn't know soldiers. As it happened, this wasn't as new as it seemed; it was a reversion to the best of American war reporting, by the great Ernie Pyle, in the Pacific theatre of operations in the Second World War. (Ernie Pyle died in action under sniper fire like so many of the GIs he made briefly famous in his reports.) The new journalism also took account of the fact that modern warfare made no distinction between soldiers and civilians, and regarded the Geneva Conventions as a dead letter. The best of it did not take sides, but neither did it share the detachment of the old journalism. It did not waste time with the vacuous juxtaposition of point and counterpoint. In my own case it took an incoming mortar to knock that out of me; but I am no politician – or at least I wasn't then. The most political I ever got was in April 1996, driving an armoured Land Rover around the looted ruins of Grbavica, the last of the Serbs' suburbs of Sarajevo to be surrendered under the Dayton Agreement. The Serbs had got the autonomy they wanted, but at a truly terrible price. This was my account of it:

> There are surely some lessons to be learned here if this ordeal is not to be repeated – important lessons, diplomatic and military. Diplomatic, that action not taken can be just as dangerous as any action being considered; that procrastination, delay, the expedient diplomatic fudge – all these can cost lives. They can and in Bosnia they have. And the military lesson is surely that, if there's no agreement between the parties, then a measure of enforcement is going to be necessary. And if you're going to threaten force you have to be willing to use force, and to bear the costs and casualties that will go with it. And if you're not willing to do that, then the best place to be is among those not present.

Those words were delivered with emphasis and respect for the ruins. They occupied a typical one minute and forty-two seconds of airtime. They were the last I ever broadcast from Bosnia for the BBC. They stood at a fair distance from the old tradition of being above and beyond the fray, but they were drawn from the well of personal experience and to this day I would stand by every one of them.

Within the BBC, the new journalism is a much broader church than the old. It includes such talents as Fergal Keane, who wears his heart on his sleeve to an extent that the old order would not have tolerated. His most celebrated broadcast, the 'Letter to Daniel', might have been more suitably placed in *Thought for the Day* than *From Our Own Correspondent*, but it was a daring and successful experiment. Fergal is adventurous with language but careful with facts. My only doubt about him is that he has something in common with Samuel Johnson: he possesses a way with words that works for him, but unfortunately gives rise to some truly dreadful imitations by others. For a while after the 'Letter to Daniel', BBC correspondents were to be found weeping into their microphones all over the world. Common sense prevailed, and the epidemic of emoting soon abated.

Between leaving Bosnia and entering politics I had a year of desuetude, in which I was out of the BBC's favour but still on its payroll. Since I had time to spare, I used it to put together some reflections on the theory and practice of journalism. These appeared in various forms: a lecture in Chichester Cathedral; a radio series called *The Truth Is Our Currency* (a phrase which I now regret having coined, since it seemed self-serving); and an article in the *British Journalism Review*. As a result, for the first time in my life, I had a pamphlet written against me.

It was called 'Whose War is it Anyway? – The Dangers of the Journalism of Attachment'. The author was Mick Hume, who was then still editor of *Living Marxism*, a lively magazine of ideas. (ITN forced it to close through a libel action that should never have been brought; in a free society, if not a Marxist one, journalists should refrain from suing each other.) Mr Hume is an original thinker and professional contrarian who makes a living by chewing up other people's orthodoxies. A piece he wrote in defence of the Bosnian Serbs was pinned up on the wall of their Press Obstruction Centre run by Sonja Karadzic, the obdurate daughter of the head of their mini-state. She did it even more damage than he did; since they didn't hold with Marxism in Pale, their capital, they blocked out the second part of the title, so that it appeared to come from a magazine called *Living* – as if it were a lifestyle offering for the fashionable set in Republika Srpska, a Balkan *Tatler* for the warlords and their ladies.

My own views on news had, I suppose, become mainstream by the 1990s and therefore a target for Mr Hume's verbal assault force. He attacked them as a threat to the truth and an attempt to turn the world's war zones into a private battleground where troubled journalists could parade their consciences and play the role of crusaders. 'What began with Martin Bell's "journalism that cares as well as knows" ends up as "who cares what we really know so long as the world knows that we care?"'[1] He was gracious enough not to charge me with prejudiced reporting – I had spent more time than most trying to understand and explain the Bosnian Serbs – but he accused me of opening the floodgates to a tide of subjective, emotive and politically partisan reporting – to which the best answer is, that it didn't happen. Today's journalists are at least as dedicated and professional as yesterday's. The likes of George Alagiah and Alan Little of the BBC and Bill Neely of ITN have thought seriously about their profession; they have indeed been trained in it as we were not, and have the sense to regard armed conflict as something more than a career opportunity. They have not gone native, and have resisted the lures of politics and polemics.

This is not to say that all is well with the fourth estate and its TV subdivision – far from it; but its infirmities are self-inflicted. They are not the fault of the reporters in the field, but the result of a failure of nerve and uncertainty of purpose at the editorial

end of the news chain. There have been some strange mani-
festations of this crisis of confidence. The most disturbing of
them are the commercial agenda and the phenomenon of virtual
news.

11

... And for Worse

The Death of News

I suspected that something had gone seriously adrift when, at the height of the Afghan conflict, ITN led its early-evening news with a still picture of the Prince of Wales in Latvia, being chided by a sixteen-year-old girl armed with a flower. The suspicions deepened when, at the turning point in the war, the BBC's *News at Six O'Clock* gave precedence to a professional footballers' strike that didn't happen over the fall of Mazar-i-Sharif that did. They hardened into certainty when the weekend news on BBC1 preferred the football World Cup draw to climactic events in Jalalabad and Kandahar. The age of trivia had not only dawned, but was already at high noon. Others outside journalism had a better sense of perspective. When the twin towers of the World Trade Center went down, one of Manchester United's footballers remarked of his profession, 'Something like this makes you realize, it's only a game, isn't it?' It was a pity that the news people lacked his wisdom.

Let's name names here. The revolution in the news agenda didn't happen by accident; it was planned. The *palme d'or* for the dumbing down of British television goes to ITN, which was once a proud name in journalism and owned half the terrestrial duopoly in TV news, until it sold its birthright on ITV for a mess of extra commercials. A spokesman for the advertisers put it bluntly: 'This is a commercial channel – it is fundamentally there to make money for itself and its shareholders, and to keep its advertisers happy.' That was its undoing. In hock to the advertisers, ITN set the trend by its decision, early in the 1990s, to promote an agenda of crime, celebrity and medical scares – and to downgrade foreign news to a couple of slots a week on Tuesdays and Thursdays, unless anything more saleable happened closer to home. Royal estrangements and divorces were a particular favourite. Pity the reporter on a distant front line who had to compete with a rumour of scandal in the House of Windsor. The judgements were not editorial but commercial – huckster television. Foreign reporting was expensive, the bean-counters argued, and it didn't attract the viewers. The change of emphasis coincided inconveniently with the start of the Bosnian war. ITN maintained a vestigial presence in central Bosnia, rather shamefacedly, as a sort of death watch – in case a British soldier were killed, and for no other reason; but it has more recently revived its interest in the world, and has suffered a disproportionate share of war-related casualties.

The BBC didn't follow the trend immediately. I belonged to the old order, and was still allowed to report real news from a real war zone for a while, in the sunset of TV news as we understood it; but by the mid-1990s the BBC's values too were sliding down-market, under the pressure of ratings and competition, on the pretext of accessibility. The watchword was 'news you can use', though 'news you can sell' was actually nearer the mark. I didn't do the lifestyle stuff, and lacked expertise as a medical reporter, so there was no place for me in the ratings-driven world of usable news. *The hell with it anyway,* I thought. *We had the audience with us in our time, we had confidence in what we were doing and our news drew higher ratings than theirs did.* After thirty-four years in the Corporation's service I suddenly had a sense of being surplus to requirements, and left for a tour of duty in the House of Commons.

Events of great consequence could not be completely ignored. Foreign news as we used to know it returned to the fray with the NATO intervention in Kosovo in June 1999, when it briefly dominated the airwaves as in the old days; but the terms of engagement were somehow different. The news people behaved like starlings on a wire. Either everyone was there or no one was. After the Milosevic regime capitulated, the mainly British ground troops advancing from Macedonia were accompanied or followed by no fewer than 2,750 journalists and their straphangers and technicians. Satellite vans clogged the highway, and patrols of the Parachute Regiment in Pristina would go out with more photographers than soldiers. Ugly scenes developed between rival reporters, and one famous BBC name pushed another into a ditch. There was a multiplicity of new TV channels, and such a media frenzy as had never happened before. The NATO commander, General Mike Jackson, did well to keep his sense of humour for most of the time, and his sanity for all of it, in the face of so great a tumult of media folk. Then, almost as fast as they had arrived, and because not enough people were being killed, the birds on the wire lost interest and went away, until the next time.

The next time was in Afghanistan two years later. In those two years the old foreign agenda had expired, not only in television. News was fluff and froth. It was whatever was reckoned by the lords of the new order in news to keep ratings and circulations from falling. It was comprehensive rubbish and palaver (there must be an acronym for that). Then Afghanistan happened. Where's Afghanistan? Who are the Taleban? What's it all about? The British people were lost in a Khyber Pass sandstorm. Our forebears, when news was telegraphed or carried by pigeon, knew more about the world in which they lived. Gladstone himself could not have conducted a Midlothian campaign amid such a cloud of ignorance, and there was no television then to raise awareness of the issues. It was before the age of microphones too. He did it by the power of the idea and the word and the voice; the only amplification he had was that he was addressing an informed electorate. A politician today, when channels multiply and streams of images cascade off satellites into living rooms, would be hard put to find an audience of a dozen, never mind tens of thousands, for a speech about atrocities in the Balkans. Atrocities in the Balkans don't fall into the convenient category of news you can use.

That the charge to the low ground was led by ITN was especially saddening, because of the commercial news service's distinguished history. Although buttressed by advertising, it had for forty years been every bit as much a public service broadcaster as the BBC. It was faster and flashier, but fundamentally just as serious. The BBC was the senior service and ITN the buccaneering one, but we sailed the same stormy waters. It was the ITN of distinguished editors like Geoffrey Cox and David Nicholas; of authoritative newsreaders like Alastair Burnett and Trevor MacDonald; and outstanding reporters like Gerald Seymour, Alan Hart (a short-lived but spectacular meteor), Michael Nicholson, Richard Lindley, Jon Snow and Sandy Gall. I was not the only BBC man to have experienced that feeling in the pit of the stomach that comes from being scooped by one of those – not often in my career, just once or twice, but it was once or twice too many. I hope that I paid it back to them at least as often. The competition was fierce and usually fair.

Those days and rivalries are gone, and a new commercial order has replaced them. It isn't the journalists but the accountants who are now in charge, and whose grey eyes scan the ledger. The old ITN had such a romance to it that I was twice tempted to join, the first time as long ago as 1969. Reporting the news was its primary objective and balancing the books was the means of making it happen; but then the priorities changed – and there is nothing romantic about news that exists to sell soap flakes. The public service remit vanished from view, and so – just a few tantalizing years short of its half century – did ITN itself. It still provided the news service for the three ITV channels, but the country's most stylish news broadcaster (an accolade that is grudgingly given but was well merited) turned into an amorphous marketing product under the label of ITV

News. The inference was that the news service didn't have to be supplied by ITN, whose credentials were well established. It could as well have been provided by Associated Newspapers or Reuters – or any news organization that could underbid for the contract. The newsreader Peter Sissons, who learned his trade at ITN and was wounded in its service, accused ITV of committing a crime against its news provider: 'ITN was one of the leading world brands in news, with a lever on the affections of the British people – and what do they do? They call it ITV News.'[1]

The end of ITN's existence was very close to happening. It fought off a bid by Sky News to supply the news service for the ITV channels at almost fire-sale prices. It did so by laying the axe to itself – shedding 200 jobs and reducing its annual budget from £45 million to £36 million. It was trying to run a news operation on half the money – not even allowing for inflation – that it had spent twenty years earlier. Foreign news was a drain on its diminished resources and therefore the first to suffer, except for the show business bureau it was planning to open in Los Angeles. The programming intentions, which could not have been signalled more clearly, sounded the retreat into soft news.

The changes were announced during a global crisis, the Afghan conflict, in which for the first time in its history successive cost-cutting had already blunted ITN's competitive edge. (The retirement of Sandy Gall, its Afghan expert, was also keenly felt.) Jon Snow, its most respected serving journalist and the anchor of Channel Four News, described the cuts as crazy, woeful and dangerous. He said, 'It's a very interesting thing that in 1991 the regulator, the Independent Television Commission, said that for ITV to produce an acceptable public service news service it should cost £55–60 million. Well, last week they announced they were going to do it for £36 million. The BBC does it for £330 million.' The BBC's dominance was bad for everyone, including the BBC.

The oddest development of all was that the Corporation, finding itself in sole possession of the high ground, felt lonely up there and chose to abandon it. The change didn't happen overnight, and strongholds of serious and reflective journalism remained in such programmes as *Newsnight*, *Correspondent* and *Panorama*; but BBC News was pioneering a downhill path without reconnaissance. As any soldier will tell you, that is a dangerous thing to do. In both style and substance it transformed itself from what it had been – the standard of good practice in broadcast journalism, and the measure by which others judge themselves – into something strange and new and unsure of itself. Its showcase was BBC1's *News at Six O'Clock*, which it changed in short order from a serious news programme into a sort of marionette show. You could wade into its depths without getting your feet wet.

A veteran political producer was dismayed to receive a note of guidance from her editor: 'Tackle the serious issues if you have to, but can't you do it with a lighter touch?' Richard Sambrook, newly installed as Chief Executive of BBC News, wrote: 'For many years the BBC has rightly prided itself on its reputation for fairness, impartiality, accuracy and authority. We are trusted and respected. However, that is no longer enough ... we have to engage audiences and tell them why the news matters ... we have to find new ways of engaging our viewers, of drawing them in.'² In an internal memorandum he announced a major financial reward for whoever could win back the lost audience. The short cut was to ignore the famines of Africa, except on rare and symbolic occasions, and devote three pages to Roy Keane's latest outburst on or off the football field. Once you go down that road, there is very little chance of turning back.

The new ways of engaging the viewers were not in fact new ways at all. They were imported lock, stock and barrel from the United States. An American style guru, one Carla Hargis, came with them, to coach BBC reporters in presentation techniques that may be all the rage at Channel 39 in San Diego, but are quite out of place in Britain. News was redefined not as a reporting but as a performing art. This was manifest nonsense. We Brits are not a demonstrative people. We prefer understatement. Except for the hucksters selling kitchen appliances, we do not by and large use hand signals on television. However, under the new regime reporters were required not only to walk and talk at the same time (a technique that I never mastered, and that is actually rather harder than it looks), but to semaphore their lines as well as speak them. The tick-tack men, redundant on the racecourse, found a use for their talents on television. Someone wrote to me, knowing of my interest in the matter, about the antics of reporters 'striding towards camera, each hand clutching an invisible leaping mackerel'.

Since the news programmes remained at their regular length, something had to go to make way for all this, and the casualty was the old-fashioned news footage, the images of what was actually going on in the world – that sense of being in the thick of things, for which a two-way interview with an actor on a rooftop is no substitute. David Nicholas, formerly of ITN, wrote to me: 'I am infuriated by the prolix, repetitious, opinionating, factless two-minuters, which pass for down-the-line interviews.' Yvonne Ridley of the *Sunday Express*, who was lucky to survive her capture by the Taleban in Afghanistan, was scathing about the TV reporters who stayed behind 'on the rooftops of the Pearl Continental in Peshawar or the Marriott in Islamabad ... some journalists became quite inventive in making viewers think that they were in the thick of the action'.[3]

The live two-way interview hijacked the news to the point where it became a waste of time and a parody of itself. In the run-up to the Second Gulf War, President Bush and Prime Minister Blair held a summit meeting in the Azores. The war was inevitable, and as a news event the summit did not amount to much more than a photo opportunity. The Americans were set on a course to war, with the British in their slipstream.

The BBC's report of the event – such as it was, all flags and soundbites – was followed by interviews with no fewer than six of its special correspondents in the Azores and across the world. There is nothing so special about being a correspondent. A correspondent is a reporter who has lunch. The outcome in this case, as in so many others, wasn't news in any known or recognizable form. It was vanity television, infected by the modern disease of correspondentitis. On any major story, the demands of the rolling news channels are so great that a reporter is assigned round the clock, with camera and satellite dish, to the role of rooftop journalist. This person is known as the 'dish monkey' or, if a woman, the 'dish bitch'.

A truthful exchange with a dish monkey, which you will never actually hear on television, would go something like this:

'Martin, would you share your insights with us on what's going on in Ruritania tonight?'

'I don't have any insights, Huw; it's pitch-dark here and I can't see a bloody thing.'

'And during the day?'

'Same story, Huw. I've been so busy answering questions from your colleagues on News 24, BBC World News, the One O'Clock, and Six O'Clock News, not to mention Radio Wales, Radio Scotland, Radio Stoke-on-Trent, the stations in Manchester and Birmingham and BBC On Line, that I have been stuck up here on the hotel rooftop all day long. I am probably the least-informed person in the whole of Ruritania.'

'You're wasting our time then?'

'Or else you're wasting mine – one or the other.'

The Reporter's Friend

In 2001 the BBC published internally a 174-page handbook, 'The Reporter's Friend', which set out the theory behind the practice. It made interesting reading, especially between the lines. To dispel the general bafflement of their viewers, they should have made it more widely available instead of just circulating it internally. Indeed, they plan to do so. The handbook's cover was like the line-up on Lenin's Tomb – a montage of photographs showing the correspondents in favour, and (by eloquent omission) those out of favour, including even the Chief News Correspondent.

The author of the landmark booklet, Vin Ray, was once my most capable field producer in Sarajevo, which would locate him firmly in the old guard of TV news; and much of what he wrote was a brave attempt to graft the old values onto the new. He was good on the clarity and simplicity that lie at the heart of story-telling: 'The most effective scripts are often quite "spare" in their style.' He had no mercy on the hackneyed phrases that substitute for thought: 'Dawn revealed the full extent of the cliché.' He tried to hold the line against gimmicks for their own sake: 'The ability to walk and talk in front of a camera may be a valuable thing – but it is worth very little unless you have something worth saying.' He introduced us to DROVUA: 'You know what that means, don't you? Sorry – I assumed you did – it means Don't Rely On Viewers Understanding Acronyms.' And he included an intriguing paragraph on 'attitude': 'If you're an absolute genius you may be forgiven membership of the tantrum brigade. Otherwise forget it.'

All of this was sound advice in the practice of TV news both ancient and modern; but Vin Ray was not only a writer and custodian of the old values – he was also a survivor and apologist for the new ones. BBC News made him its Assistant Head of Newsgathering. He therefore had to justify the dominance of live broadcasting over just about everything else in the repertoire, although I doubt whether in his heart he truly believed in it. He certainly knew its costs and pitfalls better than most.

'Live reporting skills are an absolute prerequisite for any serious correspondent these days. With the growth of 24-hour networks and the move towards "deconstructing" what would have been conventional film packages, live reporting has become important – and yet it is potentially so hazardous . . . avoid bad weather, big crowds and people with alcohol. You'll lose out to all three.'⁴

He should have added children, animals and funerals – but note that word 'deconstructing'. What was being proposed here, on a management whim and with scant regard for the consequences, was the dismantling of a tradition of presenting the news on television, crafted and developed over the years, by assembling and editing the most compelling images available – and confining the reporter to a subsidiary role, as the least significant part of the whole enterprise. (Michael Buerk's self-restraint in his report on the Ethiopian famine in 1984 was a model to us all.) In the new dispensation, a substantial proportion of such images would be jettisoned to make way for the correspondent with hand signals, and the phenomenon of journalism as a performing art: 'Reporting live involves a larger element of "showbiz" than some correspondents feel comfortable with . . . It's what actors sometimes call "being in the moment" or "capturing the moment" . . . how you look and "perform" on screen is crucial.'⁵

A larger element of 'showbiz' would be nowhere more tasteless than in the coverage of an African famine; but in a curious way, the actorishness in vogue had brought TV news full circle to where it started. My very first report on the BBC's network news, about cattle prices in Acle market in Norfolk, in 1963, was introduced from London by an actor. (I was definitely not 'in the moment', and the footage has mercifully gone missing from the archive.) Most of the newsreaders in those days were actors. They were selected for their trained voices, their clear delivery and their classical good looks; they did their job with proficiency and were highly regarded for it. The difference today is that reporters are being expected, without any of the training it takes, to become impromptu actors in their own right and on their own beats, as much in Whitehall and Downing Street as in foreign fields. The results are frequently disastrous. If that's what the management really wants, it should – like the children's programmes – recruit from the Royal Academy of Dramatic Art.

Having been a field man for thirty-seven years, I hope I can claim to be an expert viewer of these experiments – even a trained viewer, if such a category exists. I know the real thing when I see it, and I know the unreal. I don't want reporters (the men, at least) to address me from far-flung locations with make-up on their faces and not a hair out of place. Nor do I expect them to stand uniformly 'at a slight angle and leaning slightly forward' (another Vin Ray formula). I expect them to look a touch rough and rugged, with dust and sweat on crumpled safari shirts, as if they've been somewhere interesting and have a story to tell that's worth listening to. It was once said of ITN's Sandy Gall and myself that we had faces like the relief maps of the countries we were covering. The country in his case was Afghanistan and in mine it was Bosnia – neither of which is blessed with regular features; but film-star good looks were not then in the job description.

Virtual News

The reductio ad absurdum of the prevailing fashion is the video-wall. It is a full-length screen in the corner of the news studio onto which graphics, maps, photographs and moving images are projected like scatter-shot. As if to the scaffold, doomed correspondents are led to this contraption and required to make an obeisance to the newsreader, before turning awkwardly to the camera and addressing it with both hands flailing and all the gadgets flashing in the background. Not only does this fail as a device for delivering information; it is prone to extreme and career-threatening disasters. One poor soul had the autocue go down on him early in the exercise, his arms went into overdrive and he completely 'corpsed' (only the theatrical term is appropriate). The next week, he fled the country and sought redemption in a war zone.

The deeper objection to this fad is that it misunderstands and misuses the new technology. It is as if you were presented with a casket full of pearls and diamonds and used them to decorate the family Christmas tree. You can do that if you wish, of course, and produce some eye-catching and attractive effects, but it is hardly the best and most ambitious use of your resources.

The impact of the new technology – video cameras, video-phones and satellites – should be liberating. It should enable journalism of a scope and reach that was just not possible in the film and airfreight age of TV news; but there is one essential ingredient to it. It requires the reporter to be *out there*, discovering things, piecing them together, making sense of them and using the satellite to send them back in the shortest possible time frame. Whether the reporter appears at all, at whatever angle to the camera, is more or less irrelevant; the most powerful images speak best for themselves. (The older I got, I found, the more I edited myself out of it.) By contrast, the videowall reverses the process. The reporter is *in here*, talking against images of which he or she has no first-hand knowledge, which were chosen by someone else and which may be of doubtful provenance and immediacy. It is known in the business as 'wallpaper'. The result is a loss of authority and a waste of airtime.

Foreign correspondents starting out today enjoy significantly less freedom than I did, although they should have more. During the Bosnian War, one of the mandarins of the BBC newsroom regretted that he had little control over the reports that I was sending. Highly explosive events were occurring, and at some time in the course of the day he would like to have been consulted about them. It was before the age of mobile phones in war zones; but I had recently been caught up in a spot of bother and he graciously allowed me my freedom.

'You're the one being shot at,' he said, 'and I am not, so I accept that there's nothing I can do about it.'

They bided their time, and now they have done something about it. They haven't gone as far as the American networks, in demanding that the reporter's script be approved by Atlanta or New York before the editing even begins: this allows the correspondent in the field about as much freedom of action as a puppet on a string. Instead, the BBC's centre – which has its own *Pravda*-like tendencies – has asserted itself by turning its outposts into spokes of its electronic hub, where the reporters perform in controlled and almost theatrical circumstances. All the world's a TV studio, and the men and women in it merely players. They go with the show, because by doing so they secure their allotted 'glory time' on camera without earning it. I know of one correspondent who was all over the airwaves for two weeks during a crisis in Taiwan, and was thought to have performed with great success, which no doubt he did – but he never left the TV station except for his hotel. We live these days in an age of spin, as much in television as in politics.

All of this marks a sad declension from what seems to me, looking back on it, to have been a golden age of news. The broadcasters have lost the plot. They can repair the damage if they wish to, and for that they must look to the past more than the present, and to practice rather than theory. I'm not at all sure about the academic side of it, and the value of media training schemes, except in matters of libel law. It was Nicholas Tomalin of the *Sunday Times*, tragically killed on the Golan Heights in Syria in 1973, who famously remarked that all that it takes to succeed in journalism is a way with words and a certain rat-like cunning. It is one of those things that you can only learn by doing it. So you look around you, and see what works and what doesn't, which phrases soar and which crash on take-off, whose example to follow and whose to avoid, like the arm-wavers – naming names would be invidious, but they know who they are. Handbooks are helpful, but personal examples much more so.

In the absence of a day's formal training, which I never had, my role model was James Cameron, the thinking man's foreign correspondent, and roving columnist of the late and much lamented *News Chronicle*. I wept when it died. And he wasn't only mine, I discovered, he was also the role model of Robert Fisk, the *Independent*'s wild-eyed man in Beirut. Robert and I were very different sorts of foreign correspondent. We once shared an armoured Land Rover along the rutted tracks of central Bosnia, on the condition that I drove and he shut up. We both aspired to be James Cameron, and I guess that of the two of us he came closer. We met Cameron at the start of our careers and the end of his. Like Cameron, Robert Fisk had the loner's confidence not to run with the pack. It was a habit that won him few sympathizers, so that when he was nearly stoned to death by an angry crowd on the Afghan border, one of his rivals was heard to observe that he knew just how the crowd felt. The Jewish lobby reviled him as an anti-Semite (which he is not). I wrote to him one day on impulse and out of concern for his safety. The very next week he received a death threat and was deeply shocked by it. He wrote back to me, 'You have, by extraordinary coincidence, caught my own mood exactly. My hate mail is becoming incandescent – of the "you will die before going to hell" variety ... we need to fight back against these vicious, dangerous remarks.' The only two books which, in my view, should be mandatory reading in our journalism schools are James Cameron's *Points of Departure* and Evelyn Waugh's *Scoop*. The rest, including mine and even Robert's, are just memoirs.

Who are the role models for today's reporters? Perhaps Robert Fisk, or Anthony Loyd of *The Times* – who also reports in a personal, old-fashioned way, and with a sublime indifference to danger and discomfort. It's hard to see any other candidates, except perhaps the BBC's Alan Little, John Simpson and Matt Frei, all on account of their writing – and Kate Adie, on account of being Kate Adie; but she should have quit when I first advised her to, in 1995, as even then the writing was on the videowall for both of us. As Jon Snow has observed, the species is endangered: 'The thing which worries me is that the number of people who have reporting experience to draw on is beginning to diminish, which is crazy, because we never needed them more than we do now.'

We are entering new territory here, the land of the inauthentic. It is possible these days to enjoy a successful career as a virtual foreign correspondent, without actually travelling very far or doing very much or taking any risks. All that is required of you is to look sincere, apply your make-up, throw no tantrums, take your turn to be dish monkey, write fast and stay close to your communications. This last is the most important, because of the technical changes which have transformed TV news, and perhaps overwhelmed it. The journalism has fallen behind the technology. When I started my travels, in Ghana in 1966 and Vietnam in 1967, I was working with cameramen who (if they weren't retired taxi drivers, which some were) had come to us from the cinema newsreels, had carried film cans in Wardour Street, were trained in the medium of film and carried exposure meters. At the height of the riot or fire-fight their hands would disappear into black bags to change magazines. The rolls they shot were shipped to London to be processed and edited. The film had the magnetic sound track down the side of it; strips of it were glued together with Scotch tape, and sometimes fell apart on transmission. Michael Aspel made a name for himself as a presenter by ad-libbing his way out of such calamities: that was his life. The newschain of events from field to screen was frustrating, cumbersome and time-consuming, but at least from the reporter's point of view it was authentic. Those were the days of triumph or disaster. You either were there or you weren't, you had the film or you didn't. Film, unlike videotape, could not be easily copied. There was no way of covering your tracks by folding in material obtained by a news agency or friendly network operating, so to speak, in another part of the forest. I once deconstructed one of my own reports, at the usual length of one minute and forty-two seconds; it had come from a dozen different cameras, news agencies and TV networks, only one of which was mine. The ability to vouch for the truth that we told was slipping out of sight on a falling tide.

Of course, human nature being what it is, there were sharp practices and charlatans on the scene even in the age of film. It was not unknown for American correspondents in Saigon to rely on their valiant Vietnamese cameramen for the combat footage, while for their accompanying on-camera performances they would venture no further than the jungle foliage of the city's botanical gardens; but I cannot believe that our turn-of-the-century virtual news techniques have advanced the craft of broadcast journalism – indeed, they have set it back. At least the botanical gardens were real. The videowall is not.

12

War in Iraq

Straws in the Wind

In 1993, when the Bosnian War was at its height, I travelled regularly from peaceful Heathrow to embattled Sarajevo. Ten years later the roles, or at least the appearances, were reversed. The guns were silent in the Bosnian capital, the runway had ceased to be a shooting gallery and armoured vehicles were no longer prowling the streets; but London's main airport, when I passed through it on a mission to Bosnia for UNICEF, was ringed with the armour of the Household Cavalry Regiment and guards (not security guards but infantry of the Guards Division) patrolled the terminals. The British were nervous, and had plenty to be nervous about; or perhaps it suited the government's agenda to make them nervous. Intelligence reports suggested that shoulder-launched missiles had been smuggled into the country and might be used against an aircraft on the Heathrow flight path. The Prime Minister's determination to join the Americans in their assault on Iraq, with or without United Nations authorization, made the United Kingdom a likely candidate for the attentions of Islamic terrorists. The fact that the war was being launched without sufficient public support didn't make people feel any safer. Sarajevo, the historical powder keg of Europe, seemed in every respect a city more at ease with itself.

The war was unpopular. The case for it was never adequately made. The British and American governments did what they could to convince their people, through media management,

dodgy dossiers and the black arts of spin, that armed intervention was just and necessary. The tanks at the airport may
have had something to do with it too. The argument seemed to
vary according to the day of the week. First, Saddam Hussein
had weapons of mass destruction and must therefore be disarmed. Then, if the UN's weapons inspectors couldn't find
evidence of them, that also showed he was in material breach
of UN resolutions. When the Iraqis started destroying them, as
they did with the short range al-Samoud missiles, that was
dismissed as a cynical tactic to buy time and divide the Security
Council. Besides, the Iraqi leader was a bad guy anyway and
Baghdad had regime change coming to it whatever happened.
The moral high ground was contested territory; but a million
demonstrators on the streets, schoolchildren marching on the
gates of Downing Street, two massive parliamentary rebellions
and the resignation of a senior cabinet minister made no difference to Tony Blair's determination to go to war in Washington's slipstream. Amid clouds of disinformation from three
capitals – London, Washington and Baghdad – there were straws
in the wind that cried out for a George Orwell to do justice to
them.

One of these straws blew in, across the years, from the conflict
in which Orwell fought and was wounded – the Spanish Civil
War. Outside the Security Council in New York there hangs a
reproduction of Picasso's masterpiece *Guernica*, the first and
most famous artistic statement of the horrors of aerial warfare.
'Painting is not just done to decorate apartments,' Picasso said.
'It is an instrument of war ... against brutality and darkness.'[1]
The picture was a gift by the philanthropist and politician
Nelson Rockefeller. For nearly twenty years it had been the
backdrop against which ambassadors and foreign ministers,
coming and going, made their statements to TV cameras – an
appropriate backdrop too, since it showed very clearly what
follows when diplomacy fails. In January 2003, with 200,000
American troops and six aircraft-carrier battle groups on their

way to war, a blue curtain was discreetly hung in the corridor as an alternative to Picasso's painting. The Americans, who were planning the most intensive air campaign in history, objected to having their Secretary of State standing in front of the depiction of the pioneering attack by bombers on a centre of civilian population. German aircraft had used Guernica as a laboratory of incendiary warfare and had caused 1,600 casualties on 26 April 1937. The UN capitulated. Its spokesman, Fred Eckhard, explained that the blue curtain with its UN emblems was a technically better background for the cameras. There was surely something symbolic about shrouding an argument for peace to make the case for war. I have always seen myself as a Blairite – not Tony Blair but Eric, which was George Orwell's real name. Where were you when we needed you, Mr Blair?

Something similar, although altogether more trivial, happened to me on the innocuous airwaves of BBC's Radio Two. I was on the *Johnny Walker Show*, promoting my solitary venture into pop music, a hip-hop record about the dumbing down of news. Johnny Walker is a popular disc jockey with an interest in politics and a real independence of mind. He asked me about the war, to which I replied mildly that I didn't think the case for it had been made. He also talked about the record, which was frankly no musical masterwork, and he played it to its full embarrassing length of nearly four minutes. He then returned to the war.

'What's this about embedding?' he asked.

'It's when journalists are assigned to the military and sent to the war to live with the units they are going to report on. It happened to me with the 7th Armoured Brigade in 1991. But now they're not just accredited but recruited.'

'Does it work?'

'Sometimes it does and sometimes it doesn't,' I answered. 'It depends who you are, who you're with and the extent of the censorship. It worked for me, but it's a trade-off of freedom for access. I think it's OK so long as the intention of the military is to inform and not to deceive. But what's happening here, I think, is a different sort of embedding. The Alastair Campbell spin machine is being embedded into the Ministry of Defence.'

At that point a message flashed up on Johnny's computer screen. It was from his editor: 'No more questions about the war,' it said. *Don't mention the war* was a catchphrase from the immortal sitcom *Fawlty Towers*; but this wasn't the comic cosmos of Basil Fawlty: it was real-world, mainstream broadcasting. It was then that I realized, this war was going to be a tough one for the media – tougher perhaps than any before. Whether the reporters were in or out of bed with the armies in the field would make little difference in the age of manipulated news. They were in for a hard time.

The new phenomenon was the presence of the spin doctors in or close to the theatre of war. Nothing like it had happened before, except very briefly in Kosovo. These shadowy figures affected the coverage – or, initially, the lack of coverage – of the build-up of British troops in northern Kuwait. Twelve years earlier we had dealt straightforwardly with the soldiers and enjoyed almost total access: the only areas off-limits to us were deception and intelligence operations, army chaplains (for fear of upsetting the Saudis) and field hospitals (for fear of spreading alarm on the home front). This time there was a Coalition Information Centre, or Spin City, coming into being. In the early phase of the deployment access was restricted and reporters were steered away from the front-line troops and towards the cooks and postmen – as if the army's sole and sufficient purpose was eating lunch and receiving mail. The Americans were more honest and forthright. Paul Adams, the BBC's defence correspondent, reported the answer given by a US Marine, in the oddly named Camp Matilda, to a question about what they were trained to do: 'We kill people, sir,' he said, 'and we blow things up.'[2]

It was also time to say goodbye to the illusion of casualty-free conflict. In the run-up to the war a very senior British soldier, just retired, asked a question about reporters in general and Kate Adie and myself in particular: 'In the Bosnian War, when the British forces were peacekeepers and no one's enemy, not part of an invading force and seldom directly targeted, how often did you come under fire?'

'More than we could count,' was the answer, 'and more than was good for our chances of survival.'

'How do you fancy Iraq, then?' asked the very senior soldier. Given the numbers and the risks involved, it was a certainty that the casualties would include journalists. Terry Lloyd, an old friend and rival from ITN, was the first of them, killed by American fire in no-man's-land.

Endgame

The case for the use of force against Saddam Hussein, as it was argued in the Security Council in the climactic debates of February and March 2003 (and in front of the dissembling curtain outside the chamber), depended on two ideas that were entirely new to international relations. One was regime change – that one country could be justified, on moral grounds, in charging across the borders and overthrowing the government of another. The other was the idea of an unreasonable or capricious veto of a UN resolution by a permanent member of the Security Council. It was advanced by the two-nation coalition of the United States and Britain – sheriff and deputy sheriff of the new world order – as a justification for invading Iraq despite a veto threatened by France with the support of Russia, Germany and China. Sir Crispin Tickell, a distinguished former British Ambassador to the United Nations, described this approach as the law of the jungle applied to international affairs. The custom and practice of the UN required a resolution threatening 'all necessary means' to be passed before force could be used in its name. Such a resolution, which had authorized war in 1991, was not even on the table. The threat of 'serious consequences', which was on the table, didn't even come close to it. Without it the British and Americans, who claimed to be planning a war of liberation, would actually be waging a war of aggression under international law. Kofi Annan, the UN Secretary General, specifically warned them that they would be acting outside the United Nations Charter. President Bush brushed the argument aside, as the leader of the only country that was not subject to the constraints of others but could play by its own rules: 'If we need to act we will act, and we really don't need the approval of the United Nations to do so.' He also said, 'At one point we may be the only ones left ... That's OK with me. We are America.' There was something about what he said and his way of saying it that chilled the spine and left people wondering: *If there really is a rogue state out there somewhere, is its capital Washington rather than Baghdad?* And what exactly was the model of democracy that the Americans were planning to impose on the Iraqis? Robin Cook, resigning from the government on the eve of war, said, 'What has come to trouble me most over past weeks is the suspicion that if the hanging chads in Florida had gone the other way and Al Gore had been elected, we would not now be about to commit British troops.'[3]

The war was optional and the damage was self-inflicted. By doing not very much of anything internationally since September 2001, Iraq had succeeded (where the old Soviet Union had failed over a much longer period) in dividing and damaging both the Atlantic Alliance and the cohesion of Western Europe. Nato was reeling from an outburst by German Foreign Minister Joschka Fischer against American Defence Secretary Donald Rumsfeld at a conference in Munich six weeks before the outbreak of war. A sign of Fischer's seriousness was that he said what he had to say in English to his former ally and present adversary: 'In a democratic country you have to make the case, and that case has not yet been made. I cannot convince my people to attack Iraq if I myself am not convinced.' Shortly after that I ran into the Nato spokesman, Jamie Shea, at a German

Foreign Ministry conference in Berlin. We discussed the phenomenon of megaphone diplomacy, the unprecedented public outspokenness of diplomats and ministers. I welcomed it, he didn't. It made them occupy positions from which they couldn't retreat.

'What they do in public is nothing,' he said; 'you should see how they go at each other in private.'

The nightmare scenario for Tony Blair, from the start of the crisis, had been to be towed into the war by America, like a dinghy behind a battleship, without the support of a real coalition and the cover of an authorizing UN resolution. This scenario was unfolding day by day. The United States and Britain didn't make a coalition but a gang of two, a latter-day Don Quixote and Sancho Panza, armed and dangerous and tilting at oilfields. Not only was the famously persuasive Mr Blair unable to convince the smaller countries on the Security Council (some of which were post-colonial tinpot dictatorships and serious candidates for regime change themselves) of the case for a second Security Council resolution; he couldn't even convince his own people. Right up until the eve of the conflict public opinion continued to resist him. He even feared it might be the end of his premiership.

There were many reasons for this. One was the inadequacy of the shifting arguments advanced for the use of force. Another had to do with personalities. The eloquence of the French Foreign Minister, Dominique de Villepin, who opposed the war with fluency in four languages, was never matched by Washington's spokesmen, especially Donald Rumsfeld, who was spoiling for a fight and grated on European nerves by presenting Iraq as a piece of 'real estate' – that was really his term – awaiting liberation. A further reason, I believe, was a new variant of the notorious CNN effect – the phenomenon of television's impact on politics. I had a personal insight into this because, although I was determined to set foot in no more war zones, I was invited by Channel Five News to analyse the war from its studio in Gray's Inn Road: Kirsty Young's perch was a safer vantage point than a Warrior armoured vehicle. As 'A' Day and 'G' Day approached (the starts of the air and ground campaigns), the images of America's military might cascaded into the newsrooms of the electronic village – from the news agencies of Reuters and APTN, from military sources and from the cameras of other broadcasters. As with the previous Gulf War, the networks were obliged to pool their coverage. The pictures were spectacular and sensational, as if they were intended to be admired as well as feared. Set the weapons systems aside from their purposes, and aircraft carriers, stealth bombers and main battle tanks can be seen as things of beauty, clean-lined creatures of the seas and skies and sands. They were also in this case inventions of the finest minds that the dollar could buy, the extreme expressions of the art and science of warfare in the twenty-first century; and because the US defence budget didn't fall but rise with the end of the Cold War, they were the result of the Pentagon's ultimate arms race, which was an arms race with itself. This contest was mad and self-propelling, conducted out of all proportion to any threat, least of all from a minor-league Mesopotamian dictatorship. No one else could compete. The mission of all the weapons assembled in the digitized battlespace of the Gulf – Star Wars technology brought to earth – was not only to shock and to awe, but also to be tested. After all, if you had invented them, wouldn't you want to see if they worked? And where better to do so than in a country with a despotic regime, a weak defence and an abundant supply of desert? Iraq was a laboratory as well as a battlefield.

Every carrier battle group, Marine Corps expeditionary force and army formation had its camera crews and reporters in attendance, as I had been in my time, but never on such a scale and with so much firepower inviting admiration. New weapons systems had been developed since the last Gulf War, smarter missiles, bigger bombs and secret forms of electronic warfare. Almost on the eve of battle the Americans tested their MOAB, the Massive Ordnance Air Burst (also known as the Mother Of All Bombs) a 21,000 pound weapon of mass destruction that exploded above its target with the biggest bang ever made by a non-nuclear device. Rear Admiral Barry Costello, Commander of the USS *Constellation* battle group, observed matter-of-factly: 'There has never been in the history of warfare so much firepower in one place.' All this was true, but it made people wonder about the morality of using so mighty an American sledgehammer against so small an Iraqi nut. The Americans were poised to liberate the hell out of Iraq, but if there were substantial resistance, what would be left to liberate? The displays of the whiz-bang wonders of warfare were so awesome that they played into the hands of the peace party, and made the use of these weapons harder to justify or even contemplate.

Never was the frontier between television and war so intensely patrolled and contested. In the later stages of the deployment the Americans and British opened up and set out their stall of shining weapons and delivery systems for the cameras to see. Were they suddenly convinced of the merits of a free press in a free society? That's not the way of the military, to whom operational security is always paramount – and never more so than in the sandstorms of northern Kuwait on the eve of battle; but the parade of military might was not just bravado. It was a calculated part of the psychological war, waged with words as well as weapons. To a background track of 'We will rock you', the Commander of the American Fifth Fleet, Vice Admiral Timothy J. Keating, strode onto the hangar deck of the USS *Constellation* and told its cheering crew: 'Make no mistake, when the President says "Go" it's hammer time! OK? It's hammer time!' The hope, which was never realized, was to induce the collapse of the Iraqi regime without a shot being fired.

A sinister development, more dismaying than surprising, was that, at the moment when diplomacy collapsed and the war became inevitable, the stock markets, which had been in free fall for months, suddenly soared by 17 per cent in four days. The dollar surged. The *Guardian*, of all newspapers, headlined a 'Golden Scenario for Investors' – a boom time not only in the arms industry and for those companies (all American) that had already been awarded contracts for post-war construction, but in other sectors too, including oil. Rupert Murdoch, whose newspapers clamoured for war with a single voice, observed: 'The greatest thing to come out of this for the world economy would be a $20 barrel of oil. That's bigger than any tax cut in any country.' As soon as the war was over the price of petrol fell.

I'm not a pacifist or champion of peace in all circumstances and at all costs. I believe there can be such a thing as a just war. This wasn't one of them. It was obliging of the pro-war camp to set out its reasons for going to war – for killing people and blowing things up – with such candour and brutality. It would be interesting to know if Mr Murdoch's 175 editors across the world agreed unanimously with his view that an act of war is a business opportunity. If they didn't, not one of them dared to say so.

The Onslaught

Times change. Weapons and strategies change with them. In the First Gulf War there was a time lapse of five weeks between the air and ground campaigns. In the Second Gulf War that was cut to just twelve hours. The campaign started on 20 March. It was the world's first real computer war – a high-tech attack against a low-tech defence. Shocking and awful – no contest. On the second night Iraq was hit with 1,000 precision-guided missiles and bombs. The presidential compounds on the west bank of the Tigris River in Baghdad were reduced to rubble within seconds. General Tommy Franks, the commander of the mainly American forces, described it as a campaign unlike any other in history.

That much was true; but this would be no rose-strewn path to victory. A wounded American soldier remarked, 'Those star-covered Pentagon idiots promised us a victory march and flowers on the armour. What we got instead were those damned fanatics fighting for every dune.' It wasn't so much the Iraqis as the Arab volunteers alongside them who, far from welcoming the allies, offered stiff resistance in Umm Qasr, Nassiriya and most of the way until the outskirts of Baghdad. The so-called coalition was trying to avoid the soldiers' nightmare of street fighting. The British, trained in urban warfare, could do it better than the Americans. The US Marine Corps took casualties. Five of its soldiers were captured by the Iraqis and paraded on al-Jazeera television. The BBC didn't show those pictures, although it had had no qualms about broadcasting the images of Iraqi prisoners the day before. There were also casualties not caused by enemy action. An American helicopter went down on the first night of the campaign, two British helicopters on the second night and an RAF Tornado on the third, shot out of the sky by the 'friendly fire' of an American Patriot missile. When the war started, public opinion swung behind the soldiers, but doubts remained about the politicians who had put them in harm's way. The friends of one of the Royal Marines who died in the first helicopter crash left flowers with a note attached to them: 'In memory of Mark Stratford, who gave his life for this senseless war.' Those doubts were not erased by victory.

The final outcome was never in doubt; but as American spokesmen proclaimed success in the other-world of their video-linked briefing centre in Qatar, it was obvious that the campaign was not the cakewalk that Washington's ideologues had predicted. The Arab volunteers didn't play their part in the script. They greeted the invaders not with flowers and kisses, but with suicide bombs and rocket-propelled grenades. Arab fighters from many countries did not capitulate but fought back with unexpected tenacity. A British officer described two of them trying to rush his tank with hand grenades at Basra University:

'I have never seen such fanaticism. It was truly chilling.' The American ground commander Lieutenant General William Wallace admitted: 'The enemy we're fighting against is different from the one we had war-gamed against.' The lines of advance were over-extended and vulnerable to counter-attack. Any army is in trouble, as this one was, when its supply line becomes its front line.

And it still didn't look like an army of liberation. The Iraqis were either ungrateful or terrified, but until the end they showed few signs of welcoming their liberators. Imprecise bombs that put children into hospitals did nothing to convince them. Nor did a cruise missile that killed fourteen civilians in a market place in a suburb of Baghdad. You didn't need to be an old Bosnia hand to know the global impact of market-place massacres. The televised images of US Marines stalled in sandstorms and stuck in mud recalled those of Vietnam in the 1960s. A few old hands began to use the Q-word – 'quagmire' – which sent all kinds of shivers down American spines. Now as then, the enemy resisted. Now as then, the media were blamed as the bearers of bad news. Now as then, the Pentagon ordered reinforcements – a further 30,000 troops of the 4th Infantry Division and 3rd Armoured Cavalry to add to the 250,000 already in Iraq. The British Army, stretched to the limit outside Basra, could field no reserves or battle casualty replacements and had no reinforcements to send. The realization suddenly took hold that things were not quite as advertised. It was not yet a view that would pass muster on a mainstream news programme – I was hired, after all, as an analyst not a polemicist. So I put it into verse and slipped it surreptitiously into a news-paper column:

> Instead of all the flowers and cheers intended,
> An easy victory at a knock-down price,
> The politicians' optimism ended
> In friendly fire and needless sacrifice.[4]

As in the First Gulf War, the sacrifice included the victims of so-called 'friendly fire'. D Squadron of the Household Cavalry Regiment, a highly professional unit well led by Major Richard Taylor, started the war with 105 men. It lost three of them, none in combat – two to a freak accident when a Scimitar reconnaissance vehicle rolled, and the other under fire from an American A10 tankbuster, which busted the wrong side's tanks. A trooper wounded in the attack remarked: 'I am trained for combat. I can command my vehicle. What I have not been trained to do is look over my shoulder and see if an American is shooting at me.' If the casualties sustained by D Squadron had been suffered proportionately by the Americans, they would have lost more than 7,000 dead in their war in Iraq. The 'blue on blue', as it's called, was a one-way traffic. Not a single American casualty was caused by the British. Less aggressive and trigger-happy than their allies, and better at winning the peace as well as the war, they offered the Americans a model of restraint and boots-on-the-ground good soldiering. British commanders could not express their doubts about the Americans' kill-all-targets mind-set in public; but the codes were easy enough to read when the Army's senior and most admired soldier, General Sir Mike Jackson, remarked: 'We have a very considerable hearts-and-minds challenge. We are not interested in gratuitous violence.' British soldiers were appalled by the reports that went through the ranks, of American shooting sprees at roadblocks, in the streets of Umm Qasr and even in a prisoner-of-war camp. Yet, against the grain of the campaign, it was an American officer who complained against the conduct of a British commander, Lieutenant Colonel Tim Collins of the Royal Irish Regiment.

It took the Americans and British three weeks to win the war. Iraq's weapons of mass destruction, the stated reason for going to war, were never used by a regime in its death throes. Nor were they found in any deployable form. British forces were sent to war on a false prospectus. In that respect it was a fraudulent war. The vaunted Republican Guard melted away, and whole divisions of the Iraqi army surrendered without a fight. A regime which was supposed to pose a threat to the world proved unable even to defend itself: the strongest resistance to the allied onslaught was mounted not by Iraqis but by volunteers from other Arab countries: Egypt, Syria, Algeria, Morocco, Tunisia, Yemen and Saudi Arabia. One of Saddam's statues put up more of a fight than he did. It was toppled only at the second attempt.

The winners of the war were the Americans and British and the Iraqi people, who were liberated from a brutal tyranny but soon demanded the departure of their liberators. The losers were Saddam Hussein, his associates and – again – the Iraqi people, whose civilian casualties, according to hospital records, were 1,700 killed and 8,000 injured in Baghdad alone. The defining image of the war was that of a twelve-year-old boy, Ali Ismaeel Abbas, who had both his arms blown off in a not-so-precision-guided missile attack on Baghdad that killed the rest of his family. It was a picture that shocked the world and raised questions of morality and proportionality, whether the war's costs and casualties were in any way justified by its benefits. Little Ali's plight was symbolic of that of many others, including the victims of looting and disorder. It shamed the case for going to war; indeed it shamed *any* case for going to war except in circumstances of the most desperate last resort, which the war in Iraq was not; and it may possibly have made it harder for the Americans, on their next project to rearrange the world, to find allies – even the British – to go along with them. The soldiers and sailors spoke more frankly than the politicians. The retiring British Chief of the Defence Staff, Admiral Sir Michael Boyce, made clear the services' reluctance to wage another discretionary war for quite a while. Not for the first time, the soldiers had saved the politicians; but the armed forces were severely over-stretched. There were many in the military with the gravest doubts about the war they were sent to fight: too many funerals, and too many questions unanswered.

Because war is life lived at the extreme, and the extreme is where tragedy and comedy meet, this one also blended tears and laughter. It produced two media stars. One was the Iraqi Information Minister, Mohamed Saeed Sahaf, known to the tabloids as 'Comical Ali', whose announcements of the Americans' imminent defeat – 'their tanks will be their tombs' – grew ever more apocalyptic as those tanks advanced inexorably towards the Palestine Hotel where he was speaking. He understandably went AWOL on the day they reached the hotel.

Donald Rumsfeld, the American Defence Secretary and architect of the war, was equally capable of making forays into realms beyond the reach of ordinary mortals. His accounts of the war's progress would merit a PhD thesis all of their own, and certainly one well worth plagiarising. He described the days of looting and lawlessness following the fall of Baghdad, when oilfields were protected but hospitals were not, as 'untidiness'. He noted that when people were liberated they were free to do bad things as well as good. Of the repetitive rolling news coverage he said, 'When you see some person walking out of a building with a vase, you see it twenty times, and you wonder, are there that many vases in Iraq?' And he made a contribution beyond parody to the idea of the fog of war: 'As we know, there are known knowns. There are things we know we know. We also know there are known unknowns. That is to say, we know there are some things we do not know. But there are also unknown unknowns, the ones we don't know we don't know.'[5]

The 'Embeds'

The new way of war-fighting, which was a high-tech evolution of blitzkrieg, introduced a new term to war reporting: the 'embed'. Embedded journalists were not just accredited to but incorporated within individual military units. More than 600 of these conscripted scribes and snappers were deployed into the desert or on warships in the Gulf. Most of them were British and American, with a scattering of Australians, Spaniards and Italians, depending on their government's degree of support for the so-called coalition. Access was denied to all others, except those already in Baghdad as the front lines rolled towards them. One thousand seven hundred journalists were left languishing in Kuwait City with little to do but complain about their exclusion.

The first casualty was candour. This was the fault not of the embeds but of the editors, who yielded to pressure to describe the Americans and British as 'coalition forces'. This suggested the kind of broad alliance that had been assembled for the previous Gulf War, including even the Syrians and Egyptians; but the war was fought by a grouping of just two nations at the sharp end, plus a few Australian special forces. To call them a coalition was a supine misuse of language.

The embedding of journalists was a bold experiment that confounded many predictions, including my own: that it would muzzle the press and deliver only news that pleased the Pentagon. The censorship was applied with a lighter touch than in the previous Gulf War. Most of the embeds were reporting their first war, and it did them no harm to experience the realities of soldiering at first hand. Audrey Gillan of the *Guardian* was won over by the gentlemen of the Household Cavalry Regiment, and they by her; they called her their 'little packet of morale'; the Regiment's Commanding Officer recommended that his soldiers' families read the *Guardian* – and that had never happened before in the history of a regiment where, previously, to have been seen reading the *Guardian* would have threatened an officer's career! The embeds also enjoyed a degree of protection by being folded into armoured units. Ten of the twelve reporters who died in the war were non-embeds working unilaterally outside the system. Three of them were not only killed but targeted by the Americans – two in the Palestine Hotel and one on the roof of the al-Jazeera office in Baghdad.

Among the hundreds deployed, there were a few gung-ho types who saw themselves as the shock troops of the Pentagon's information war. Perhaps 'henchmen' would be a better word. It was certainly one of their favourites, as in 'henchmen of the evil dictator Saddam Hussein'. Among any group of war reporters, there will always be a few sad and pitiable wannabe soldiers – camp followers of the career they never had. Not only the younger embedded journalists, but some of the older hands as well, failed to grasp the difference between being *with* an army and being *of* an army. If they were taken prisoner, it might turn out to be quite an important, life-saving distinction for them to make. Instead, they tended to get carried away by the excitement of going to war. They had the latest in communications equipment, just as the soldiers had the latest in weapons systems – an interaction that glamorized the conduct of warfare while masking its costs. You saw the outgoing fire, but not the incoming; the winners but not the losers; the soldiers but not the civilians; the living, but not the dead. One of the American TV reporters, charging north with the 3rd Infantry Division on the second day of the war, boasted live on his network: 'This is historic television! This is historic journalism!' Whether or not it was historical, it was certainly hysterical. When CNN asked me to produce a video essay on the coverage of the war, I included it as an example of over-the-top reporting. Unfortunately the reporter concerned was one of their front-line stars. My piece was too subversive for their taste; but then, facts are subversive. CNN, under pressure from its flag-waving competitor Fox News, had drifted into a view of the war that was at odds with that of millions of its viewers. I took it as a battle honour to be censored by CNN.

Anyone can report a victory. A test of good journalism is what it says when things go wrong. (It was William Russell's Crimean question: 'Am I to tell these things, or hold my tongue?') One of the embeds who told these things was William Branigin, an experienced *Washington Post* correspondent

attached to the US Army's Third Infantry Division. He described
the killing of seven Iraqi women and children in a bus at a
roadblock near Najaf. He quoted an officer, Captain Ronny
Johnson, shouting at his troops: 'You just ······· killed a family
because you didn't fire a warning shot soon enough!' It was to
the credit of the system that Branigin's pooled report wasn't
censored, although few papers except his own chose to use it.

A less experienced embed was Chris Ayres of *The Times,* who
was taken away from his normal beat, which was to report on
Hollywood stars and celebrities, to go to the war with a US
Marine Corps artillery unit. He was alarmed to discover that
his commanding officer had been sent a directive on 'How to
deal with a dead media representative'. 'My objectivity was shot
to bits,' he wrote; 'all I wanted was for the Americans to win
quickly.'⁶ Ninety miles south of Baghdad the Marines came
close to being ambushed by twelve tanks of the Republican
Guard and were saved by the timely intervention of two F15s.
He reported the main supply route's vulnerability to counter-
attack, for which he was vilified as a 'piss-poor journalist' at
the Marine Corps' field headquarters.

Most remarkable of all was the coverage of an NBC cameraman, Craig White, who doubled as a reporter when his
correspondent, David Bloom, died of natural causes compounded by stress in the second week of the war. Outside
Baghdad his unit of US Marines ran into an ambush, which
they barely survived. White's vivid, raw, blood-and-dust footage
showed a Marine firing back while his wound was being dressed,
and a sergeant trying to drive away a blazing ammunition truck
to save his men. Craig White showed the reality of war without
gloss or glamour. 'It makes your teeth rattle,' he said. That was
the authentic voice of someone who had been there. War really
does make your teeth rattle.

The war to end all wars has never yet been fought and never
will be. So the next war is not an 'if' but a 'when'. When it
happens, and certainly if it involves the British and Americans,

the technique of embedding the press will be practised again, with the control and censorship calibrated according to how it is going. It is surely better than the alternative, which is secret wars glimpsed only through cockpit videos and distant briefings. Reports like Craig White's provide a kind of reality check against which the claims and communiqués of a one-star general on a 'podium of truth' can be tested; but they are only a particle of a fragment of one side of the story. They need to be supplemented by alternative sources, unembedded journalism, webcams and websites, new networks and new voices like those of Abu Dhabi television and al-Jazeera. Independent witness from the other side of the lines is more necessary than ever; and it is more dangerous than ever, in a world where it is safer to fight wars than to report them.

13

Afterthoughts

Imperial Echoes

It helps to understand the connectedness of things. In politics there are no free-standing events. *Actions have consequences.* Everything connects. Everything casts shadows. Regime change in Iraq was not an issue in the American presidential election of November 2000. It was an intellectual plaything of the neo-conservatives, a long-standing item on their wish list, but not a slogan on any candidate's lips. Hardly a single voter gave it a single thought; but the Second Gulf War, which was fought with that objective, was an outcome of that election. If Ralph Nader had not stood against Al Gore and split the liberal-left vote; if a few hanging chads in Florida had hung otherwise; if the decision of a politically appointed Supreme Court judge on the election's validity had gone the other way; if the events of 11 September 2001 had not lit the fuse for a war of revenge – then many thousands of people would still be alive who are now dead. Some of those people were British and Americans. The vast majority were Iraqis who lost their lives as a result of events beyond their horizon and half a world away from the country where they died. Their fate was not their fault.

Those events were also the outcome of a singular failure of politics at home. Tony Blair's decision to take the country to war gave the Americans a show of international legitimacy for what would otherwise have been (and may well have been anyway) a unilateral and unlawful war, unauthorized under the United Nations Charter. It would also set them on course for further pre-emptive wars against regimes and tyrants of their choosing. It was the greatest mistake in an otherwise charmed political career, and the most dangerous decision by a British prime minister since Anthony Eden's on Suez in 1956 – even more so, because the Americans who restrained us then were taking us with them now down the slippery slope from one war to another, as the candidates for regime change presented themselves in the New American Century. Tony Blair for once was not responding to an opinion poll or focus group. He did what he did because he believed it was the right thing to do, and he believed that he could hold the Americans in check. Unlike Margaret Thatcher's determination to go to war in the Falkland Islands in 1982, it was not a decision taken fully and collectively by the Prime Minister and Cabinet. In a post-war speech to the 7th Armoured Brigade in Basra, he described it as 'my decision to order the action'. His ministers were required to endorse it – and only one of them, Robin Cook, declined. There was nearly another, but the International Development Secretary, Clare Short, changed her mind for no reason that she ever adequately explained, before she too left the Cabinet. Power does the strangest things, even to principled people.

Until March 2003, Tony Blair had been a moderately popular and successful prime minister; but his style was presidential and power flowed into his inner circle rather than out of it. On this issue of war and peace he ruled alone. Strange things can happen to those who rule alone: they stop listening; they become prey to their own convictions and delusions; they believe in their own charisma and powers of persuasion; they become alarmingly Messianic; they look forward to meeting their Maker with an untroubled conscience. The columnist and former MP Matthew Parris wrote a series of acutely observed wartime columns. In one of them he asked: 'Are we witnessing the madness of Tony Blair?' His answer stopped short of the full affirmative, but he noted some worrying symptoms in the Prime Minister, such as saying things that were palpably absurd, and 'that fierce, quiet intensity which, from long experience of dealing with mad constituents, I know that the slightly cracked share with the genuinely convinced'.[1]

Madness was in the air. Nations, like people, can be subject to fits of dementia; and nations, like people, can be blissfully unaware of their affliction. The most enduring effect of 11 September was the unhinging of America. Early in the crisis, the novelist John le Carré attracted much opprobrium from across the Atlantic when he pointed this out: 'America has entered one of its periods of historical madness, but this is the worst I can remember: worse than McCarthyism, worse than the Bay of Pigs and in the long term potentially more disastrous than the Vietnam War.'[2] Those who supported the war saw its militarily successful conclusion as justifying the enterprise – which was another way of saying that might was right. In a contest between the Americans and Iraqis, with a thirty-year technology gap between the weapons systems of a superpower and those of a former Soviet client state, there was only ever going to be one military outcome, and that outcome duly came to pass. Even as it did, the Americans were looking for the next 'rogue state' in which to apply their novel doctrine of pre-emptive warfare. Syria and North Korea were on the candidates' list. A strong case could have been made for Zimbabwe, a rogue state with a rogue head of state, except that it lacked oil wells and strategic importance in the American view of things. So the roads to Damascus or Teheran looked more likely paths for Washington's ascendant ideologues. They had been on the fringes of power in an earlier Republican administration – Ronald Reagan's; they were the authors of the influential 'Project for the New American Century', and were now near enough to the centre of power to seek to turn their Project into reality. It is work in progress, and they are not yet done with it.

The landscape ahead of us is an unmapped minefield. If you think that where we have come from was dangerous, it is like Disneyland compared to where we are going. To wage regime-

changing wars in two Islamic states in a first term of office is an
unprecedented record for an American president. It jangles the
nerves of the rest of the world about what he might intend in a
second term. There is probably no country on earth, with the
exception of China and the Russian Federation, whose regime
could not be changed by force if the Americans chose to change
it. Certainly every nation in Europe, including both its nuclear
powers, would be vulnerable. *Now thrive the armourers ...*
There is a global shortage of Tomahawk cruise missiles. Send in
the Iron Horse (4th Mechanized Infantry Division) and the
Screaming Eagles (101st Airborne) backed by six carrier battle
groups of the US Navy, 20,000 bombs and 10,000 missiles,
MOABs and JDAMs and all the bloody alphabet of war, and
just about anything becomes possible militarily. You might not
wish to have such a war waged in the name of your freedom.
Your dissent would not count for much. You would either be
liberated or killed, depending on the precision of the bombs. As
Vice Admiral Keating declared on the USS *Constellation*, 'When
the President says "Go", it's hammer time!' In the new world
disorder, the President's hammer can be wielded at any time and
any place of his choosing. 'At any time and any place of his
choosing' was a phrase coined by his speechwriters for his first
speech after the fall of the Twin Towers, in the unlikely setting
of Washington's Episcopalian Cathedral. Now we know that it
was more than a phrase: it was a programme of action.

Might is no more right when there is only one superpower
standing than it was when there were two. It is in the nature of
empires – the Roman, British and Soviet being the outstanding
examples – that their military power will expand until it is
checked. Their peripheries will twitch and override their centres.
They will develop in the ways that empires do, in the dynamic
application of force against counter-force, whatever the orders
transmitted down their chains of command. The local commanders respond to uprisings and challenges and act accord-
ingly. That is a lesson as old as the one learned by the British in

India. There is no reason to suppose that the American empire will be any different, whatever its professions of democratic intent and its reluctance to hoist the Stars and Stripes over its new dominions, give or take a few falling statues. The only difference lies in its military might without precedent. At the start of the twenty-first century there is nothing in the world to check it, no countervailing force of sufficient strength. The next nine largest industrial economies do not collectively match the Pentagon's defence budget. Only now, in the aftershock of the war in Iraq, are we waking up to the perils of living in a world in which a war can be waged for no other reason than that it can be won, whatever the cost in civilian casualties. *Smart weapons aren't as smart as they think they are.* This is a wake-up call – what the soldiers call reveille, when they stand to in their trenches and shell-scrapes before dawn. It is time to understand the threat to us all. And to be moderately afraid.

Those threatened include the Americans themselves in the rolling wars of regime change. They are at risk not only in the obvious sense – that their enemies will be provoked to strike back at them at home and abroad. This has already happened and will continue to happen, more than they know, wherever they set up their Hiltons and McDonalds, their contractors' compounds, or their military bases and stockades. They are less secure today than they were before the fall of the Twin Towers. They are also at risk in the sense that, in asymmetrical warfare, the killing comes at a cost to the killers, who by their very manner of waging the war can be included in the ranks of its victims. Remember the words of the beleaguered Colonel Collins of the Royal Irish: 'I know of men who have taken life needlessly in other conflicts. I can assure you they live with the mark of Cain upon them.'

At the height of the war in Iraq, in a battle to isolate Najaf, American commanders called for air strikes partly out of an aversion to mowing down Iraqis with direct fire:

'There were waves and waves of people coming at them, with AK-47s, out of this factory, and they were killing everyone,' says Lieutenant Colonel [Woody] Radcliffe. 'The commander called and said, 'This is not right. This is insane. Let's hit the factory with close air support and take them all out at once.' For some soldiers, trauma is already sinking in. 'For lack of a better word, I feel almost guilty about the massacre,' says one soldier privately. 'We wasted a lot of people. It makes you wonder how many were innocent. It takes away some of the pride. We won, but at what cost?'[3]

Checks and Balances

The world has not known such unchecked power for many centuries. The Americans hold dominion over palm and pine to a degree that the British aspired to, but never quite achieved, even at the high point of their empire; nor is there an American Rudyard Kipling, a poet of empire, to write a transatlantic 'Recessional'. Rather quaintly, the actor and sage Sir Peter Ustinov blames himself, in part, for the present state of affairs. When I met him at a UNICEF event in Berlin, he set out an intriguing theory. The George Bush generation came of age at a time when his two Roman epics, *Quo Vadis?* and *Spartacus*, were widely screened in cinemas and on television. Although the parts that he played in them were hardly heroic in the Hollywood sense, these movies offered a simplified view of history and a romantic image of the last time when a single superpower bestrode the known world. Seen in this light, George Bush's America becomes the new *imperium*; but it is a fair guess that the Roman Senate was a more effective deliberative assembly than its twenty-first-century successor on Capitol Hill.

It says much about the state of the American Congress, and of the American press, that mainstream resistance to the imperial project was led by two octogenarians. Both harked back to earlier times when the power of the White House was subject to constitutional restraint and critical scrutiny. Both remembered the Tonkin Gulf resolution of 1964, with which Congress had been deceived into supporting the Vietnam War. Before, during and after the war in Iraq, President Bush's most consistent critic in the Senate was Senator Robert Byrd, the eighty-five-year-old veteran from West Virginia. 'I weep for my country,' he said on the floor of the Senate on the day the war began. 'What is happening to this country? When did we become a nation that ignores and berates our friends? When did we decide to risk undermining international order by adopting a radical and doctrinaire approach to using our awesome military might? How can we abandon diplomatic efforts when the turmoil in the world cries out for diplomacy?'[4]

In the White House press room, the lonely senator's dissent was matched by that of Helen Thomas, eighty-two-year-old doyenne of the press corps, who had been White House correspondent for the United Press for fifty-seven years, before switching to be a columnist for Hearst Newspapers. Starting with Dwight Eisenhower, she had reported on the policies and personalities of nine presidents before this one. 'I have never covered a president who actually wanted to go to war,' she said. 'Bush's policy of pre-emptive war is immoral – such a policy would legitimize Pearl Harbor. It's as if they learned none of the lessons of Vietnam ... The international world is wondering what happened to America's great heart and soul.'[5]

While others toed the Administration's line, Helen Thomas went for its jugular. It wasn't her American-Lebanese descent that gave her a perspective that differed from theirs; it was just her nature. I remembered, from my own years in the White House press room, that she was always the one to ask the awkward questions:

Ms Thomas: Why does he [the President] want to drop bombs on innocent Iraqis?

Mr Fleischer: (the White House spokesman): Helen, the question is how to protect Americans, and our allies and friends ...

Ms Thomas: They're not attacking you.

Mr Fleischer: ... from a country ...

Ms Thomas: Have they laid a glove on you or on the United States, the Iraqis, in eleven years?

Mr Fleischer: I guess you have forgotten about the Americans who were killed in the First Gulf War as a result of Saddam Hussein's aggression then.

Ms Thomas: Is this revenge, eleven years of revenge?[6]

For her dissent, Helen Thomas received a peculiar and bureaucratic punishment by seating plan. She lost her seat at the front of the press room and was relegated to the back. Better than the Gulag – but still no way to treat a living legend.

What happened to the rest of the media was something to be wondered at. It still is. They surrendered to pressure and prejudice. The headlines, even in the British press, were at times little more than cartoons. They featured the demonized caricatures of the Saddam regime – 'Chemical Ali', 'Comical Ali', 'Mrs Anthrax' and 'Dr Germ'. Thomas Friedman, a serious columnist for the *New York Times*, observed: 'Saddam Hussein is the reason God created cruise missiles ... So if and when Saddam pushes beyond the brink, and we get that one good shot, let's make sure it's a head shot.'[7] And Thomas Friedman was supposed to be vaguely on the liberal side of the argument. With liberals like Mr Friedman, who needed conservatives?

The British debate, in both press and Parliament, was more level-headed and democratic. Tony Blair is a conviction politician, but not a House of Commons man: he spends less time in the House than any of his predecessors, shows little interest in its proceedings and has the worst voting record of any prime minister in memory; he commands so many other votes that he doesn't need his own. In four years as an MP, I saw him only twice in the division lobbies (there are two of them, one on either side of the Chamber, and perhaps I was too often in the Opposition lobby to come across him more frequently); but on this issue of war and peace, it was to his credit that he did not sidestep Parliament, acting first and seeking a mandate later, as he had with Operation Desert Fox, the bombing of Iraq in 1998. On 18 March 2003, two days before co-launching the war, he put it to a vote that he could have lost; and if he had lost, or failed to carry the majority of his party with him, he and Jack Straw, the Foreign Secretary, would have resigned – or so they said later. With much arm-twisting, by the whips and even the Prime Minister's wife, the number of Labour MPs against the war was held down to a total of 139. How many more would it have taken to force his resignation? The best guess was about 200. The forty-one who didn't defect will doubtless be rewarded by patronage and promotion, which is the way with party politics. Jack Straw said later, 'It was one of those things that would have been obvious, had we arrived at that point, that we had not carried the Party. It would have been a matter of sentiment.' He confessed to some 'very dark moments' before the vote.[8]

A Post-Heroic Age

I wrote at the outset that we have no heroes but only celebrities. In the light of the war in Iraq I would like to amend that. It did produce a scattering of heroes, both in uniform and out of it. Those in uniform include Major Richard Taylor and D Squadron of the Household Cavalry Regiment, to whom this book is dedicated. Those almost in uniform included the embedded journalists William Branigin of the *Washington Post* and Craig White of NBC News, whose reports were models of truthfulness under every kind of pressure to shade the truth. Those out of uniform included the local staff of UNICEF in Baghdad, where children were dying in such numbers that they were being buried in the garden of the Saddam Paediatric Hospital, but where the agency's teams still operated although their offices had been sacked and looted: 'Three of these teams worked throughout the bombing, fighting, looting and chaos. They travelled across the city repairing and maintaining generators, and even assisted some hospitals with their generators to make sure that at least a limited amount of power was provided for the city's vital infrastructure. We applaud their courage and dedication.'⁹

Iraq was the cradle of one of the world's great civilizations from Babylon to Baghdad – poetry and sculpture, writers and artists, astronomers and mathematicians, and legends of folklore from Aladdin to Ali Baba – while we Europeans were barely out of our caves. Andrew Motion, the Poet Laureate, alluded to this in his wartime poem 'Regime Change', which spoke for the nation, as a Laureate should, in expressing its disenchantment:

> Advancing down the road from Nineveh
> Death paused a while and said, 'Now listen here.
> You see the names of places roundabout?
> They're mine now, and I've turned them inside out.'

The antiquities and the civilization were eroded by the sandstorms of the desert, by war and misrule, and finally by looting. Iraq had been reduced by twenty-seven years of dictatorship, twelve years of sanctions and three weeks of war, to a state of utter savagery. Of the ransacked treasures of Mesopotamia, Robert Fisk lamented: 'We may weep over Dresden. But over the past eight weeks, the extent of cultural loss in the land where civilization began cannot be measured in tears. Part of ourselves has been destroyed, part of humanity. We had been warned. And we did nothing.'¹⁰

The Anglo-American intervention did not improve, but actually worsened, the condition of the people. The looting did more damage than the war – a thousand times more, according to the administrator of Basra's Maternity Hospital. An odious dictatorship was toppled, to be replaced for months with nothing but chaos and misery. It was thirty-seven years since I had first set foot in the war zones. In that time I had seen whole towns reduced to rubble, churches destroyed and national treasures vandalized. Only in Basra did I ever see a looted orphanage.

It happened in the early days of the war. Because of the dangers, most of the thirty boys in the city's Number One orphanage were staying with their extended families. Four of them had nowhere to go, and were still in the building when the looters attacked it. They threw hand grenades into it at night and stole everything they could move – chairs, beds, fittings, fans and even the kitchen sink. One of the boys, Ibu, hid behind the water tank until the looters found him as they emptied it. They let him live but set fire to the children's workbooks. And regime change was supposed to be liberation . . .

The epidemic of looting raged across the city. The entire industrial area was stripped bare until only the skeletons of factories remained. For day after day, the bits and pieces of a functioning society were carried away on donkey carts by looters, who became known as the Ali Babas – except that there were more than forty thieves: there were thousands of them. The pumps of the water boosting station were dismantled for spare parts and looters' markets flourished at street corners. Even the sanitation system was a target, and lakes of sewage seeped to the city's surface. The headquarters of the education authority were ransacked every day for thirty days. The electric cables were gouged out of the walls. All that remained, blowing in the wind, were old examination papers with questions about the forty-seven wisdoms of Saddam Hussein, and how the Iraqi army would liberate Palestine. The British and Americans had a plan for war, but not a plan for peace. They protected the oil wells, but not the schools and libraries and hospitals. One of the teachers cried out in despair, 'We need a government. I don't care if it's Kurdish or Sunni or Shiite or even British, but we must have a government!' Then he paused for a moment and added, 'Any government but Saddam Hussein's!'

The aftermath of war brought together two of Iraq's great legends. The cave of Aladdin, the great vaulted atrium of the Basra Sheraton Hotel, was looted day after day by the self-described Ali Babas. It wasn't just criminality; it was a sort of revenge and reckoning. Iraqis believed, with some justice, that they themselves had been the victims of looting; their wealth had been stolen from them by a predatory regime for more than a generation. The war waged by the British and Americans gave them the chance to take little bits of it back, and to sell them for what they would fetch on the looters' market.

Courier for UNICEF

It was the plight of 'Little Ali', the maimed twelve-year-old with 60 per cent burns on his body, that brought home the realities of the war in Iraq to the people, and especially to the children, in the countries that had chosen the military option. Television, even after its self-censors have been at it, is a powerful medium for communicating distress. The children of Manchester organized a fund-raising drive, through UNICEF and the local newspaper, to help the children of Basra – a city of about the same size but with more rain and less peace. I acted as a courier between them, carrying cards and messages of sympathy from the children of the Russell Scott Primary School in Denton, in Manchester, to those of the Yomoma Girls' School in Basra. Here was a sample: 'I am sorry your school has been knocked down' (Kate); 'I hope flowers grow in your garden soon' (Chloe and Molly); 'I am a child like you who goes to school and we are sending our love and support to you' (Rebecca).

The Iraqi girls drew pictures for me to take back – not in colour, because they had no crayons, and not on drawing paper, because they had no drawing paper, but on the tattered and lined pages of old exercise books. I had expected their pictures to be of guns and tanks and burning houses, as is usually the case with children who have lived through a war. Without exception they were pictures of peace – houses and flowers, palm trees, riverboats, mosques and minarets. The reason was that under the old regime they had been required to draw the guns and soldiers of Saddam's armed forces. Half their time was spent in indoctrination; every day began with a chorus of praise for Saddam and the Ba'ath Party. It was as if lessons started in Manchester with an oath of allegiance to the Great Leader, Tony Blair; the Prime Minister has presidential tendencies, and the way things are going they may come to that, but it hasn't happened yet!

The great gain, from the children's point view, was that they no longer had to waste their time chanting 'Long live Saddam Hussein!' and 'Long live the Ba'ath Party' at the beginning of every day of their school lives. In all other ways they were worse off than before. They were living in a lawless society. Their schools had been looted or destroyed. Every day brought casualties from unexploded mines, shells and cluster bombs – and the victims were usually children, whose energy and curiosity put them in harm's way. They were hungry and unprovided. A teacher held up the remains of a pencil ground down at both ends.

'And this is a pencil of children?' she cried. 'Why? The children have no uniforms – why? They have no milk – why? This is a rich country,' she said, 'but these children are hungry. The British and Americans are taking our oil – why, why, why?'

The war in Iraq had been justified to public opinion in Britain and America, without consistency or coherence, as some kind of a response to the threat of Islamic violence. Instead it increased the threat, fomented the violence and endangered the people in whose name it was fought. In the lawlessness and deprivation of post-war Basra, it was possible already to see the conditions that incubate the plague of terrorism. To plan for war but not for peace was the greatest mistake of all. It left a residue of acrimony and anger. A British aid worker, driving through the chaos, said bitterly of the Americans, 'Basically, they're going to do the same thing they did in Afghanistan – declare it sorted and bugger off.'

The children of Basra deserved better than to suffer from such a war. So did the children of Manchester, or anywhere else, than to have it fought in their name, to protect them from dangers that turned out not to exist. We cannot afford such misbegotten wars. We cannot afford to conduct ourselves abroad in a way that requires us, at home, to surround our Parliament with concrete blocks like a fortress. We cannot afford to endanger our people on a whim about regime change, and a lie about weapons of mass destruction. We cannot afford political decision-making that is so disconnected from the views of so many, and especially from the idealism of the young. We cannot afford the unloosing of the Ali Babas, not only on the failed state of Iraq, but on the structures of the United Nations itself. We cannot afford to plan for war but not for peace. We cannot afford the establishment of an us-against-the-world 'Alamo macho' as a ruling principle in international affairs. We cannot afford any further episodes of the Anglo-American imperial adventure. We cannot afford a future like our past.

I am sometimes asked: after where I have been and what I have seen, do I not despair for that future? Actually, I don't. Not even now, after the ill-judged war in Iraq – especially not now, since the gravity of the crisis has been a wake-up call to us all. What it has shown us, yet again, is something that has been increasingly borne into us on the flood of events: that politics is too serious a business to be left to the politicians alone. They are just not to be trusted with it. They represent us, but are not representative of us. Machine politics is conspicuously part of the problem. Experience – illuminated week after week by the mock hostilities of Prime Minister's Question Time – shows that those who practise it cannot be relied on to behave democratically, sensibly, reasonably and peacefully. Tony Benn was making a valid point when he quipped that he was leaving Parliament to go into politics. He has been as influential outside the House of Commons as in it. People listen to him, because he has something to tell them that they're not hearing from the practising politicians.

The remedy lies in our hands. I am confident that one result of the present emergency, which has not ended with the war in Iraq but has only intensified with it, will be the re-engagement of the people in the political process. *Things don't always go from bad to worse.* The decision-making has become so remote from us and gone so awry, that we now understand we cannot go on like this, or if we do, it will be at our greatest peril. There is at least the possibility of a long-awaited democratic revival, either inside or outside the party system. It would be much better inside. We have seen it expressed so far outside, as a sort of anti-politics – in the uprising of the young against the war, in the peace marches, in the environmental movement, in the success of Independent mayoral candidates and single-issue parties. This is just the start of it. There is every incentive and every need for it to extend its reach into the powerhouses of the political parties. Either that, or they atrophy and die, being coalitions only of the old and the ambitious. I make the same point tirelessly (or tiresomely) at students' unions and the like, to groups of people who have, unlike myself, more future than past. They have only one life to live, and if they wish the creeps and the cranks to ruin it, all they have to do is nothing, and the creeps and cranks will duly oblige them. The choice is between making a difference and filling a space. Filling a space sounds the more comfortable option, but is without doubt the more dangerous.

An additional benefit is that our dangers and discontents have taught us anew what not to take for granted. It is the original question, with which I started this journey into world disorder, of whether we live in a golden age or a fools' paradise. I still incline to the fools' paradise theory, but defer to the wisdom of my grandfather, Robert Bell, whose collected poems,

Afterthoughts, were published in 1929. One of them is called 'Illusion':

> The white house glimmers through the trees:
> The grave and gentle candles shine.
> 'Here, surely, here at last is peace' . . .
> Perhaps he thinks the same of mine.[11]

Notes

Introduction

1 The *Guardian*, 9 April 2003.
2 ITV News, 8 April 2003.
3 *Henry V*, II, i.

1. The Clash of Arms

1 Max Sebald, *On the Natural History of Destruction* (translated by my sister, Anthea Bell), Hamish Hamilton, London 2002, p. 27.
2 David Rohde, *A Safe Area*, Simon & Schuster, London 1997, p. 360.
3 Ibid., p. 353.
4 Milos Stankovic, *Trusted Mole*, HarperCollins, London 2000, p. 168.
5 Roy Jenkins, *Churchill*, Macmillan, London 2001, p. 681.

2. The War of Words

1 Speech to the Royal United Services Institute, 9 July 1999.
2 Speech to a German Foreign Ministry conference, Berlin, 20 February 2003.
3 Roy Jenkins, *Churchill*, Macmillan, London 2001, p. 778.
4 Rudyard Kipling, *The Irish Guards in the Great War*, Spellmount, Staplehurst 1997, p. 233.
5 Bob Woodward, *Bush at War*, Simon & Schuster, New York 2002, p. 139.

6 Ibid., p. 322.
7 Ibid., p. 107.
8 Ibid., p. 108.
9 Ibid., p. 211.
10 Ibid., p. 295.
11 *Daily Telegraph*, 21 February 2003.

3. War, Lies and Videotape

1 Edmund Blunden, *Undertones Of War*, Richard Cobden-Sanderson, London 1930, p. 97.
2 Ibid., p. 264.
3 *War And The Media*, Sage Publications, London 2003, p. 233.
4 *The First Casualty*, André Deutsch, London 1975, p. 223.
5 *The Kindness of Strangers*, Headline, London 2002, p. 331.
6 *The First Casualty*, André Deutsch, London 1975, p. 81.
7 'Anthem For Doomed Youth' (written 1917), by Wilfred Owen.
8 The *New York Times*, 25 March 2003.

4. Living with Terrorism

1 *Masterminds of Terror*, Mainstream, Edinburgh 2003, p. 168.
2 Ibid., p. 36.
3 Ibid., pp. 198–201.
4 *The Reporter's Friend*, BBC News 2001, p. 134.
5 *Understanding Terrorism*, Sage Publications, London 2003, p. 294.
6 *Washington Post*, 16 October 2002.
7 *Masterminds of Terror*, Mainstream, Edinburgh 2003, p. 159.

5. 'Take Me With You, Please'

1 *News From No Man's Land*, Macmillan, London 2002, p. 270.

6. Malawi

1 Speech to World Health Organization conference, 1 April 2003.
2 UNICEF press release, 4 March 2003.

7. Yesterday's Wars

1 *New News, Old News*, Independent Television Commission, London 2002, p. 98
2 *Daily Telegraph*, 28 August 2002.
3 *Daily Mail*, 10 December 2002.

8. Party Politics

1 *Keeping it Clean*, IPPR, London 2002, p. 34.
2 Speech in Prague City Square, 1 January 1990.
3 Draft Guidelines of the Electoral Reform Society's Commission on Candidate Selection, 2003, paragraph 34.
4 *Independent Member*, Methuen, London 1959, p. 373.
5 See note 3: 'Draft Guidelines ...', paragraph 12.
6 Hansard, 13 February 2002, column 243.

9. The Evil That Men Do

1 Niklas Frank, *In the Shadow of the Reich*, Alfred A. Knopf, New York 1991, p. 356.
2 G. M. Gilbert, *Nuremberg Diary*, Farrar Straus, New York 1947, p. 4.
3 Gary Jonathan Bass, *Stay the Hand of Vengeance*, Princeton University Press 2002, p. 25.
4 The *Guardian*, 19 December 2002.

10. Journalism for Better ...

1 *Whose War Is It Anyway?*, Informic 1997, p. 27.

11. ... And for Worse

1 The *Observer*, 1 September 2002.
2 *The Reporter's Friend*, BBC News 2001, p. 6.
3 *War and the Media*, Sage Publications, London 2003, p. 249.
4 'The Reporter's Friend', BBC News 2001, p. 128.
5 Ibid., p. 134.

12. War in Iraq

1 Nicholas Rankin, *Telegram From Guernica*, Faber and Faber, London 2003, p. 3.
2 *From Our Own Correspondent*, BBC Radio 4, 2 March 2003.
3 Hansard, 17 March 2003, column 728.
4 The *Mail on Sunday*, 30 March 2003.
5 Pentagon briefing, 12 February 2002.
6 *The Times,* 11 April 2003.

13. Afterthoughts

1 *The Times*, 29 March 2003.
2 *The Times*, 15 January 2003.
3 The *Christian Science Monitor,* 11 April 2003.
4 Speech in the Senate, 20 March 2003.
5 Speech at the Massachusetts Institute of Technology, 6 November 2002.
6 White House press briefing, 6 January 2003.
7 *New York Times*, 6 November 1997.

8   *The Times*, 26 April 2003.

9   UNICEF situation report, 17 April 2003.

10 The *Independent*, 3 June 2003.

11 R. Bell, *Afterthoughts*, Methuen, London 1929.

Index